HORSES OF THE WORLD

THE WORLD OF NATURE
HORSES OF THE WORLD

Edited by
PAMELA MACGREGOR MORRIS
and
NEREO LUGLI

ORBIS PUBLISHING·LONDON

The photographs in this book were supplied by:
Animals: 37 a (Bradley Smith), 114 b, 121 b, 125 b –
Archivio I.G.D.A.: 8, 10 (C. Bevilacqua), 69 –
Atlas Photo: 55 b (Doumic), 84 b (D. Colomb) –
Bavaria-Verlag: 48 (H. Pfletschinger), 81 (H.
Schünemann) – P. Bertrand: 55 a, 60 b, 64 –
C. Bevilacqua: 11 – Buzzini: 54, 60 a – Camera
Press: 78 – C.E.D.R.I.: 16, 43 (Frastier), 52, 53 a, 90,
91 – Bruce Coleman: 23 a (G. D. Plage), 23 b, 75 (J.
Burton), 121 a (S. C. Bisserot), 122/123 (J. Van
Wormer) – A. C. Cooper: 6 – Farabola: 104 –
Giraudon: 14 – L. Giusti: 105 – GP & Rom: 12 –
W. L. Hamilton: 39 – I.C.P.: 1–3, 7, 9 a, 24/25, 50,
65, 66/67, 72, 74, 76, 79, 94/95, 113, 114 a, 116/117,
119, 124 – M. Leigheb: 33 b, 40, 111 – E. R.
Manewal: 110 – Marka: 22, 49, 51 a (V. Wentzel),
82 (E. G. Carle), 118, 125 a (Grant Heilman) –
T. Míček: 37 b, 88, 93, 96 – A. Nekam: 98–100 –
Novosti: 101–103, 106–109 – Olympia: 57, 58/59 –
E. Östman: 5/6 (I. G. Gilchrist), 87 b, 89 (V. M. D.
Franzson) – M. Pedone: 45 – P. Popper: 33 a, 34/35,
38 (T. Sheppard), 41, 77, 115 – Pubbliaerfoto: 13 –
Publifoto: 62 – W. W. Rouch & Co.: 70, 71, 73 –
Scala: 9 b – S.E.F.: 36 a, 63 – Shostal: 120 –
J. Six: 28–31, 36 b, 61 – Tiofoto: 51 b, 83 –
A. Trouché: 44, 46, 56, 97 – Z.E.F.A.: 47 (H. Lütticke),
53 b (E. M. Bordis), 80 (B. Heydemann), 84 a
(K. Biedermann), 86 (W. Ferchland), 87a (W. Lummer),
126 (Shostal) – Z.F.A.: 85, 92.

Printed in Italy by IGDA, Novara
ISBN 0 85613 146 6

Based on the Italian *Il Cavallo*
edited by Nereo Lugli

Because the horse is international, the only variable from country to country is man's attitude towards him. Since the time of the Roman gladiators and before, horses have been bred for sport in many parts of the world, and this book will undoubtedly have a wide appeal in countries whose tradition is steeped in racing, trotting, three-day events and show jumping. It traces the evolution of the equine species and the distribution of the various types of horse throughout the world, in two main divisions—the warm-blooded horse, from which the riding horse has been developed, and the cold-blooded horse which produced the draught animal. The main part of the book is devoted to an exhaustive description of the various breeds throughout the world, profusely illustrated in colour by a series of unique and original photographs which were taken especially for this purpose, and many of which show the horses in their natural wild surroundings.

The renaissance of the horse as a pleasure animal, only a few decades after his decline as a utility animal with the coming of the internal combustion engine, has resulted in a universal revival of interest in riding, both for its own sake and as a competitive sport. With the rapid increase in leisure, and the growing opportunities given to the young in an affluent society, this interest is widening every year. More and more people are riding, and their numbers are drawn from every walk of life.

I believe that the more civilized and progressive a country becomes, the greater the need of its inhabitants to relax in the countryside, as far removed as possible from steel, concrete, crowds and diesel fumes. On the back of a horse one is able to escape still further from the noise and bustle of modern living, and the hundreds of pony-trekking centres that have sprung up in the last decade enable many people to enjoy riding in unspoiled surroundings, though their previous experience may be negligible, on quiet animals ideally suited to the novice. The more ambitious will graduate to more active forms of horsemanship and horses more plentifully endowed with courage and temperament.

In many countries horses are still bred and used for all kinds of work, as they have been for centuries: the climate, environment and the particular needs of the people have combined to produce many famous individual breeds. Other types of horse have evolved to meet the requirements of different sports, such as racing, trotting, show-jumping and polo. In another vein, the beauty and spirit of horses are indispensable in such entertainments as the circus and the rodeo. The horse, in fact, having fought for bare survival through the centuries, has now won its biggest battle of all – its fight with civilization.

This book is not only an outstanding work of reference but an enjoyable one to dip into—the sort of volume, in fact, which is more likely to find its way onto the bedside table than to remain on the bookshelf, and one which will appeal to novice and expert alike.

Pamela Macgregor-Morris

Contents

Index of breeds

The horse in history and today

The description of the horse as being 'the noblest conquest of man' by the French naturalist, Buffon, is one of many famous quotations in the same vein pertaining to this splendid and remarkable animal who is in many ways a paradox – at the same time bold yet timorous, possessed of great physical strength and yet willing, even eager apparently, to allow himself to be dominated and controlled by man.

While Buffon's words reflect man's traditional and long-standing admiration for the horse, they fail to do justice to an animal that has proved, throughout history, to be his most faithful and valuable ally. Shakespeare's King Richard III expressed the extreme value of horses to man in his urgent cry: 'A horse, a horse, my kingdom for a horse!'

Since the horse was domesticated, thousands of years ago, it has shown a singular ability to adapt to the uses of man, playing a major part in fields as diverse as commerce, war and sport. This contribution towards the development of man drew

A pause after a long and difficult birth. Within half an hour the newborn foal will get up and explore this strange new world.

The meet: hunting has been a popular sport in England for almost two thousand years.

A handsome grey shows off his beautiful colours in the sun.

the following tribute from John Trotwood Moore: 'Wherever a man has left his footprint in the long ascent from barbarism to civilization, we will find the hoofprint of the horse beside it.' Some historians even hold that all the great civilizations in early times developed among horse-owning and horse-using nations, while those in which the horse remained unknown or untamed remained stagnant, making no contribution to the advancement of mankind. Such was the impact of the horse upon early civilizations that the figure of the man on horseback was recognized as a symbol of power. Art, literature and poetry have all paid tribute to the unique qualities of the horse, which put him above all other animals.

Although today the man on horseback no longer represents political strength, he still cuts a fine and distinguished figure. The horse has been

ousted from many of its former fields of operation by the machine. Its proud record in war, trade and transport has been brought to a halt in the twentieth century and is unlikely ever to be restored. Yet the horse is neither declining in popularity nor dying out – quite the reverse. It has simply changed its role, adapting to the various requirements of man.

Having diminished with alarming speed during the 1940s, the equine population is once more increasing all over the world. Not only this, but the quality and beauty of the best specimens of horse have been improved, as have the number of distinct, pure breeds. Action is being taken in many countries to save those species that are in danger of extinction, and to restore those that have recently disappeared from their natural environment. At the same time, man continues to

3

cultivate, through selective breeding and enlightened training, the horse's prized qualities of speed, endurance and ability in various fields for the purposes of sport and recreation. It is in these areas now, after all, that the horse attracts the maximum popular attention.

When organized horse racing – one of the most widely patronized spectator sports in the world – developed on modern lines some two hundred years ago, attention was lavished upon one particular breed, the Thoroughbred, which was adopted as the English racehorse in the eighteenth century, and thereafter by almost all the major horse racing nations of the world. Perhaps the glamour attendant upon racing – 'the sport of kings' – contributes to the widely held view that the racehorse represents the nearest thing to perfection in the world of horses.

Yet, just as every ideal depends upon contemporary circumstances, so this concept of perfection has no absolute justification. Every horse, every breed is sovereign in its own environment. The majestic power of the Percheron or the swift grace of the Camargue pony are arguably more beautiful than the thoroughbred to those who appreciate them, and they are certainly better suited to their respective habitats of rich arable land or wide, treacherous marshes. The elegance of the Thoroughbred would be of little value pulling into his collar beside the sturdy Shire horse in the ploughfield, just as the strength and stamina of the Vladimir would be useless on the racecourse.

What is a breed?

History and environment create the horse which interprets and represents them. Breeds of horse derive according to the wishes of man, expressed in selective breeding to produce a definite type of animal, or as the result of a long process of natural selection. Some types, indeed, such as the Palomino, are not really breeds at all, but might more properly be termed varieties. But the economic necessity for producing, and then safeguarding, a particular characteristic – even if it be only colour – has induced man to separate, select and reproduce different breeds.

Authorities agree that each animal group shall be called a breed when it is able to pass on particular, superior characteristics of its own. Each breed, moreover, tends to establish and perpetuate

The sturdy Welsh Cob has the muscles of a horse packed into the size of a pony.

George Stubbs (1724-1806) was one of the greatest painters of horses of all time, and indeed was known as 'The Master of the Horse'. Here are Scrubb (above) and Bay Malton.

Show-jumping at Royal Windsor. The greatest height ever jumped by a horse (Huaso) in the ring was 8 ft 1¼ ins, in Chile in 1949.

these characteristics. Nature is the first to defend this principle, letting the strongest, the purest and the best adapted breeds oust those which are less capable of mastering their environment. This is the well known principle of the survival of the fittest.

So tyrannical a law of nature might seem to preclude or inhibit the establishment of new breeds. But climatic changes, the exhaustion of food supplies, the appearance of a natural enemy or the ravages of a disease which has not previously been encountered may from time to time effect changes in the environment. In this case, herds of horses may migrate towards new regions; if they remain in their normal environment they must adapt to changed conditions, or establish a resistance to new diseases. They are the new dominant strain, and the founders of a new breed.

The evolution of the horse

The horse that has served man so ably for the past four thousand years is *Equus caballus,* a species whose history dates back a million years. No living representatives of this species can be described as truly wild; those horses which roam free and graze in certain territories are really feral, which is to say that they are merely the descendants of once-domesticated horses that managed to escape. The other living members of the horse family – asses, onagers, and zebras – are placed together with the domestic horse in the genus *Equus.* Another species in this genus, the Quagga, only finally became extinct in about the mid-nineteenth century.

The history of the horse family affords a fascinating study, made all the more intriguing by

7

the difference of opinion which exists over such matters as the location of the original species and the pattern of equine migration throughout the world. There is little doubt, however, that the horse and its relatives underwent their most significant evolutionary changes in North America. The evidence upon which this theory is based is provided by the remarkable series of fossil skeletons discovered in the trans-Mississippi area of the USA at the beginning of the present century. These fossils have enabled archeologists and other scientists to reconstruct the history of the horse in minute detail, finally accounting for a period spanning some fifty million years.

The history of the Equidae begins with *Eohippus*, the so-called 'dawn horse' which lived during the Eocene epoch about fifty million years ago. Its habitat was the forests of North America and Europe, where it lived and behaved very much like the mouse deer of the present era. Its appearance bore little resemblance to that of the modern horse, and it was consequently some years before researchers came to the conclusion that a link existed between this rather odd little creature and *Equus caballus*.

Eohippus was essentially a primitive animal, no larger than a Labrador retriever. While its teeth were characteristic of the early mammals, it possessed a unique feature in the arrangement of its toes, with four on the front limbs and three on the rear.

The progression towards the modern horse was carried a stage further during the subsequent epoch, the Oligocene, with the appearance of *Mesohippus* and *Miohippus*. The most significant developments were in the structure of the teeth and feet; both genera had three toes on both fore and hind feet, and fully developed premolar teeth – a state of affairs which did not last long, in evolutionary terms.

The early Miocene epoch, about twenty-five million years ago, represents a watershed in the evolution of the horse family. The descendants of *Miohippus* divided themselves into two distinct groups; the *Anchitheres* and the *Equinae* (the true

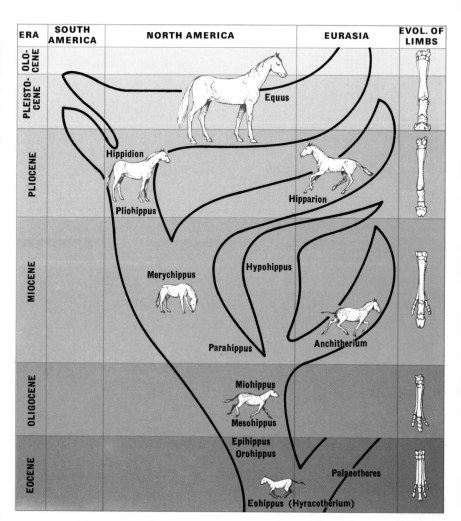

Above: The most important stages in the evolution of the horse. Its height changed from just under 1 ft to 6 ft 6 ins and more; the five 'fingers' merged into one hoof; and the teeth became adapted to eating grain and grass rather than leaves. The head became straighter and the eyes were set wider apart.
Below: The first page in the history of the horse, drawn on the walls of a cave at Lascaux, in France, between ten and twenty thousand years ago. The drawings at Lascaux – in the Dordogne region – illustrate hundreds of animals, as well as these compact, furry-coated ponies. All of these creatures were hunted by the primitive men whose artistic achievements miraculously survived the centuries, providing us with an invaluable record of life in their time.

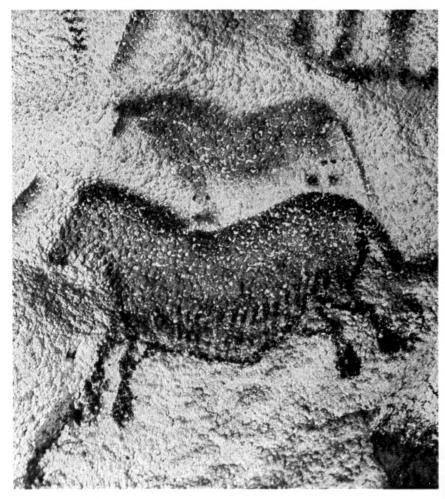

8

A young Appaloosa, with unusually large markings.

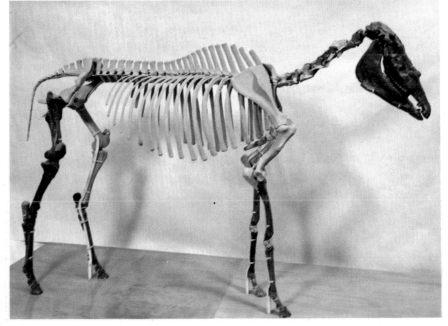

A reconstruction of Equus Stenonis, *found a hundred years ago in the Arno valley in Italy.*

horses). The destiny of the horse was bound up with the latter subfamily: the *Anchithere* line, after spreading from North America to Europe, became extinct about ten million years ago, at the end of the Miocene epoch and during the early stages of the Pliocene.

The progression of the *Equiniae* owes itself to two inter-related factors: the appearance of grasses on the American plains during the Miocene epoch, and the subsequent gradual development of teeth suited to this rich new food supply. This was evident among *Parahippus* and the more advanced genus, *Merychippus*. The latter soon developed teeth which resembled those of the modern horse: long and sufficiently durable to withstand a lifetime's wear. At the same time, significant changes were taking place in the shape and size of the limbs, together with an increase in

Assurbanipal (seventh century BC*), hunting lions in his chariot.*

The favourite horse of the ancient Greeks was the Arab.

10

overall size. The final appearance was similar to that of the modern pony.

The descendants of *Merychippus* formed no fewer than six separate lines. Of these, only two are of any historic importance: the *Hipparion* and *Pliohippus*. The former, though well adapted to grazing, became extinct in the late Pliocene. The latter, an all-important line, was typified by an animal almost identical in form to the horse as we know it today, and it is in fact through this line that the *Equus caballus* was evolved. The transition from *Pliohippus* to *Equus* is estimated to have taken place about a million years ago, at the end of the Pliocene epoch.

Equus caballus spread from continent to continent, reaching Asia and Europe via natural land bridges of continuous ice and earth. Yet neither this widespread migration, which continued uninterrupted for the next 250,000 years, nor the Ice Age which followed, account for what is regarded as the most extraordinary event in the history of the horse family – the complete extinction of horses throughout the entire North American continent.

The disappearance of *Equus caballus* from its birthplace remains an unsolved mystery. The horse remained unknown in America until the modern animal was successfully reintroduced there by the European colonists of the sixteenth century. Indeed, the horse was a primary factor in the conquest of Central America by the Spanish: the native Indians, never having seen a man on a horse before, imagined this to be some supernatural creature and fled before him in terror.

A big question mark

With the disappearance of the horse from the North American continent, the destiny of the genus *Equus* was left in the keeping of the four varieties that had survived the Ice Age, which

11

ended approximately ten thousand years ago. These four varieties – horses, onagers, asses and zebras – were distributed in an oddly representative fashion throughout the length and breadth of the Old World, with the horses occupying an extensive belt north of the mountain ranges that span the width of Europe and Asia.

The wide variations in climate, altitude and soil found within this vast territory undoubtedly played a part in the development of the horse over the last ten thousand years, and account for the remarkable differences in size and shape among the present equine population. Broadly speaking, cold climates and mountainous areas tend to produce a small, stocky variety, which we know as the pony, while hot climates favour a larger and more elegant horse. Wet climates and lush pastures produce slow, heavy horses, while dry areas, with less grazing, promote a lighter, more mobile type.

It is these environmental factors, together with the subsequent intervention of man, that have influenced the development and distribution of the horse over this long period of time. They have, moreover, helped to establish and perpetuate those features which we regard as being characteristic of the individual breeds and types of horse that are found in the world today.

While environmental factors and the breeding records of earlier horse-owning and horse-using nations provide us with a fairly clear understanding of the development of the horse, considerable doubt still prevails concerning the precise ancestry of the modern breeds. Whether or not the present-day breeds descended from a common ancestor remains a matter for conjecture,

but it is generally agreed that a great number derive from two horses which survived the Ice Age – namely Przewalski's horse, which still exists, and the Tarpan.

The former is believed to be the only true wild horse remaining in the world today. Having originated somewhere in the region of the Asiatic steppes, Przewalski's horse lived for thousands of years in the Gobi Desert. Over the years, the herds were drastically reduced in numbers as man killed or tamed specimens that were captured in hunts. Today, Przewalski's horse – a compact, dun-coloured pony with an erect mane – exists mainly in the zoos of North America and Europe; the last wild herds survive on a remote mountain range on the borders of China, but they are believed to number less than a hundred specimens at the present time.

The Tarpan evolved during the Stone Age, and, like Przewalski's horse, was hunted by man for thousands of years. It lived in a wild state in the Ukraine and in eastern Europe until the end of the last century, when the animal became extinct. Nevertheless, it is claimed that some specimens of the Tarpan still exist, in a semi-wild state, in certain European nature reserves, though their pedigree is very doubtful. Experimental breeders, like those at the famous Munich Zoo, have all the same managed to restore, by careful selective breeding, the peculiar characteristics of the wild Tarpan – the dorsal stripe and the black mane and tail.

The Tarpan and Przewalski's horse have been credited in the world of horses as being the probable and original progenitors of the Arabian and other Oriental breeds. It is through these

Eastern horses that the Thoroughbred and almost all other improved breeds of modern times have descended. All present-day breeds which trace back to the Tarpan and Przewalski's horse are collectively entitled 'warm-blooded' breeds – a term which does not refer to blood temperature but to the existence of Eastern blood in their pedigree.

The other major division of horses, the 'cold-blooded' breeds, are derived from the Forest horse, a heavy animal, which gave rise to the modern Norwegian Dun. This horse, which dates back to prehistoric times, survived the Ice Age and flourished on the rich pastures of Europe; it was first domesticated about three thousand years ago. From this horse was bred the famous Great Horse of the Middle Ages, familiar to us from paintings of knights in armour, which in its turn contributed to the ancestry of the modern heavy draught breeds of northern Europe.

The distinction between 'warm-blooded' and 'cold-blooded' breeds is often fine, since there are many modern breeds which possess warm and cold blood in almost equal proportions. These horses are perhaps best classified as intermediate breeds.

Oriental breeds

Since its discovery by the European nobility during the Crusades of the twelfth and thirteenth centuries, the Oriental horse became the most coveted prize of the horse-using civilizations. The speed, agility and elegance of the Oriental breeds made a lasting impression on all who saw them, and it was not long before vast numbers were imported into England, France and Spain. In subse-

The Circus Maximus in Rome, built by Tarquinius Priscus (616-579 BC), was used for chariot racing until the final defeat of the Ostrogoths by Belisarius in AD 549. It was rebuilt and enlarged many times, and at the time of Pliny the Younger (AD 61-114) it had a capacity of 300,000 spectators.

The Eastern warriors fought with bow and arrow, and rode heavy horses from Persia, or from Asia Minor as shown here.

quent years they were interbred with the native domestic stock of these nations, producing the various breeds of light horse which exist throughout the world today.

In previous years there was some doubt as to the identity of the original founder member of the group. Each individual breed – Turkoman, Persian, Syrian, Arabian, Barb (Barbary) – had some claim to consideration as the progenitor of the others. Recent archeological discoveries and ancient texts seem to justify the most widely-held and traditional theory, which places the Arab breed at the foundation of the whole group. Even if the Roman historians were in ignorance of its existence, it already inhabited the mysterious desert peninsula of Arabia at the time of the Roman Empire, existed in the days of the Queen of Sheba, and may be traced back as far as four thousand years.

The Arabian is the head of a far-flung family and the part-ancestor of almost all the improved warm-blooded breeds that are in existence today; even the Barb, that other noble representative of the Oriental horse, has some Arabian blood. In terms of its breeding, the Arabian is regarded as being perfection in itself. Undoubtedly the best improver is Arabian blood, which is to be found in 75 per cent of the most important breeds. It takes fifteen generations to cancel out a single induction of Arab blood.

The Arabian is a horse bred in absolute purity, without recourse to any other breed; and it has been bred within the same family for thousands of years, right up to the present time.

The horse and man

Once established in the Old World the horse was, for a long period, beyond the reach of primitive man. Its speed, the vigilant watch of the stallions who guarded each herd, its acute senses and its strong instinct of self-preservation and survival saved it from every stratagem and surprise attack. It was only towards the Upper Paleolithic, twenty to thirty thousand years ago, that man succeeded in mastering such coveted game by locating the movements of seasonal migration to carry out large scale massacres.

The men of the Stone Age hunted many types of horse for food. Perhaps the greatest massacre of all time took place at Solutré, a small settlement in the Saône-et-Loire in France. The bones found at Solutré cover an area of some three miles. The evidence obtained from this ossuary makes it highly likely that man once stripped the meat from his victims, made small cuts in the cleaned bones, and sucked out the marrow. The horse hunted at Solutré was 13 to 14 hands in size (1 hand = 4 inches) and did not differ greatly in appearance from Przewalski's horse.

The hunting of horses continued in Egypt and certain other nations until about 1000 BC, but it is clear that by this time other peoples had already begun to use, rather than to kill, the horses that they caught in the wild. Certainly the existence of domesticated horses was recorded as far back as 2500 BC, and it is believed that horses were being used for a variety of purposes in the Eastern Hemisphere by 1000 BC.

Nevertheless it is not known precisely where, and by whom, the horse was first domesticated. The few records and references that do exist suggest that the first horse-masters were nomads of central Asia, who may have begun to ride and breed horses some centuries before 2500 BC. It is unlikely that the small horses of the nomads were used for draught purposes. Indeed, they may well have been simply herded like cattle, and maintained as a source of milk and meat and hide.

Further support of the view that the horse was first domesticated by the Asian tribes is provided by the records of the Aryans' conquest of northern Europe, India and Persia. The Aryan nation, four thousand years ago, occupied a vast area which is now called Asiatic Russia. It seems unlikely that this great people could have carried out the conquest and occupation of these areas without the assistance of horses, which they had previously domesticated and adapted for service in war.

The earliest horse owners were not slow to realize the potential of the horse. At some stage in the Bronze Age the art of basic riding was mastered by the peoples of northern Asia, and thereafter the horse adapted itself rapidly to the many requirements of man. By the end of the Bronze Age, some three thousand years ago, the horse had become dominant in one vital area of human endeavour – the sphere of war. One important distinction, first alluded to in the texts of the Old Testament, had already become apparent: the horse was 'the animal of war, as the ass was of peace.' That distinction was to remain valid for thousands of years.

The horse in war

The hoof is a miracle of anatomy, with an infinite number of veins, shock-proofing devices and different textures.

Since its first appearance on the battlefields of the ancient world, the horse has influenced the course of history to an incalculable degree, shaping the destinies of many nations. In this respect the history of the horse is therefore very close to the history of the great horse-owning nations of the world.

The horse made its debut in the arena of war drawing a chariot. The supreme exponents of chariotry were the Hittites, a people of eastern Turkey, who imported both horses and the very best types of chariot from the Mitanni. Under the Hittites, the combination of chariot and horse was destined to revolutionize the art of warfare.

Within the space of three hundred years the Hittites created a military empire covering the greater part of Asia Minor, and even sacked Babylon – achievements which owed much to the horse. The rapid striking power and mobility of chariotry had dramatically overturned the balance of power in the ancient world.

Chariotry remained the most important feature of armies for the greater part of the pre-Christian era, but was destined to disappear almost as dramatically as it had emerged as the nature of warfare altered once again.

The decline of the chariot, and its eventual shift from the arena of war into the racing arena, became inevitable in the face of increasing use of missile weapons. The unprotected charioteer was at an immediate disadvantage against well-disciplined infantry. Armies consequently channelled their energies into the creation of a more flexible force, which, if adequately protected, could operate within a relatively close range of enemy infantry.

Their efforts were given further impetus by the greater availability of riding horses, bred in increasing numbers. The combination of the horse, now used as a charger, and the armoured warrior gave birth to a new and revolutionary phenomenon: the cavalry.

The Assyrians may have been the first people to employ cavalry – they are also reputed to be the first to maintain records of horse breeding. At the height of its power, Assyria was able to field an army of some sixty thousand men, of which about two thousand were mounted. The precise role of the Assyrian horseman remains unknown, but there is no doubt that other nations, among them Macedonia, Persia and Greece, employed their horsemen as cavalry during their conflicts. It seems likely that these Eastern horses lacked stamina at first, for each mounted warrior had a spare lead horse as well. The riders rode bareback, sometimes with a square of cloth beneath them, sitting well back with their knees up, their legs pressed round the horse's flanks and their heels tucked in just in front of the stifle joints. The soldiers were either archers or spearmen.

Diagram labels: fetlock, bulb of heel, cleft of frog, sides of frog, pastern, frog, toe of frog, coronet, wall of hoof, toe, quarter, bulb of heel, heel, angle of wall, angle of sole, sole, laminae, toe

The bits were primitive and often severe jointed snaffles, adorned with spiky protruberances both inside and outside the mouth. The saddle with a tree to protect the horse's spine from the weight of the rider did not appear until late Roman times, and the stirrup, which finally made the rider secure in the saddle, did not appear until about the sixth century AD, when it spread westwards in gradual stages until it reached France two centuries later.

Having replaced the chariot as the most mobile form of attack, cavalry enjoyed an unrivalled supremacy in battle for a virtually unbroken period of 1,400 years. At no stage in that period was that supremacy more decisive than in the decline of the Roman Empire.

The Romans, while renowned in the breeding of horses for sport and recreation, depended largely on their heavily-armoured infantry in the field of battle, with their cavalry, such as it was, fulfilling merely an auxiliary role. Rome paid a heavy price for its exaggerated reliance upon infantry. Over the course of two hundred years, Roman armies fell successively to the Persians, Goths and Visigoths, and in each case the superiority of the invaders' cavalry proved to be the decisive factor.

Despite the success of lighter and faster horses in the campaigns of the Huns under Atilla, the Magyars and the Mongols, heavy cavalry became the order of the day in medieval Europe. The Goths and the Vandals from north Germany started to breed and ride heavier horses by the second and third centuries AD, following the example of the Persians, whose horses (though only 14 hands in height) were said to have feet that 'shake the earth'.

The Barbarians bred their horses from the heavy Forest horses of Scandinavia and north Germany. The Goths fought from their Baltic home right into southern Russia, and the Vandals swept across Europe from north Germany and down into north Africa. Two hundred years later the Lombards, a third Teutonic nation, were also mounted on heavy chargers, and swept down into Italy. By the thirteenth and fourteenth centuries the cavalrymen in light chain mail, fighting on lightweight horses, had been replaced by the armoured knights on heavyweight chargers, also protected by armour. These cold-blooded horses, among them the legendary Great Horse, were predominant in the successive small wars of the period.

With the development of firearms in the fourteenth and fifteenth centuries, armies were forced to think again on their choice of horse for cavalry units. The combination of heavy charger and bulky armour, so effective for so long, was no match for the mobile infantry equipped with firearms. Indeed, in 1346 at Crécy the Welsh bowmen had already cut the French cavalry to pieces. Gradually the armies of Europe turned their attention back to the lightly-built and speedy horses that had been bred from the Eastern stock imported after the Crusades.

This new type of war horse was at its best in the great European armies of the seventeenth and eighteenth centuries, a period in which the great traditions of the cavalry were born. Under Louis XIV and Frederick the Great, cavalry reached new heights of efficiency, due to the superior mobility of the lighter breeds used by both monarchs. The improvement continued through the reign of Napoleon, under whom the cavalry became the élite of the French Army, although it was the infantry that carried out the greater part of the fighting. In England, as on the Continent, the glamour and prestige of the cavalry held a particular attraction for the nobility and the landed gentry, and it was from these privileged sections of society that the large majority of cavalry officers were recruited.

The colour, style and panache of the British cavalry regiments, coupled with their success in the defence of the Empire, undoubtedly contributed to the belief, widespread in the nineteenth century, that cavalry was invincible in the field of battle. Yet it was clear to many progressive observers that the cavalry was becoming outmoded as increasingly sophisticated weapons were developed. With the introduction of automatic weapons in the late nineteenth century, the role of cavalry became the subject of bitter controversy.

The pessimism of earlier observers was borne out by the passage of events in the two World Wars of the present century. The first of them, with its extensive trench warfare, offered no opportunities for the use of cavalry, except in eastern Europe, where only small units were employed. Any hopes that remained of a revival of the cavalry were to be mercilessly crushed at the start of the Second World War, when the brave resistance of the Polish cavalry was simply swept aside by the German Army. The ease with which the German infantry and their tanks destroyed one of the finest cavalries in history was conclusive proof that the horse had no place in modern warfare – a fact which, although it signalled the end of a brave tradition, was a merciful release for the horse himself.

Small cavalry forces were and are still maintained by various armies all over the world, chiefly for ceremonial purposes. It is not without significance that cavalry units were involved in the

Horses have to be shod on average every six weeks, and a blacksmith's skill is much sought after and requires long training. These pictures show various stages in the making and fitting of horseshoes.

17

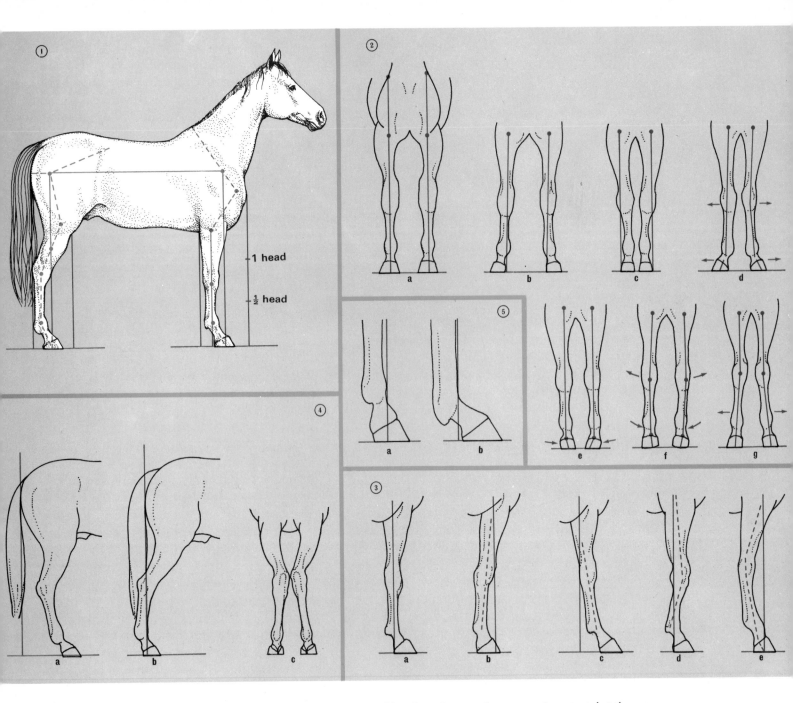

The points of balance—the limbs of the horse compared against a vertical line from the ground—are most important, but the same defects may not be as damning to one breed as to another, and may even turn to a horse's advantage. (1) Normal points of balance on the fore and hind legs, in profile, and shown in proportion to the head. (2) Forelegs seen from the front: a, normal; b, wide-chested; c, narrow-chested; d, splayfooted; e, pigeon-toed; f, bow-legged; g, knock-kneed. (3) Legs seen in profile: a, normal; b, back-standing; c, front-standing; d and e, calf-kneed. (4) Defects of the hind legs: a, front-standing; b, sickle-hocked; c, cow-hocked. (5) Defects of the hoof: a, straight jointed; b, long-jointed.

last actions of both the First and the Second World War; but with the disappearance of the horse from active combat after more than two thousand years, the proud record of the horse in war came to an end.

The origins of racing

The Romans were the greatest specialists in horse breeding in early times. They bred horses for the mail, horses for use on the farms, hunting horses, war horses and, above all, horses for sport. The horses used in the famous circus races at the Colosseum and elsewhere were imported from Mauritania and from Syria, from Libya and Asia Minor. These horses, with their Oriental blood, were the ancestors of the present-day racehorse.

At the Circus, a crowd of over 100,000 spectators filled the various orders of seating or standing arrangements, while slaves sold programmes and some of them accepted bets and wagers. One could place a bet in one's absence, and at the finish of each race a pigeon was released with a list of the results attached to a claw. With the fall of Rome, the races were continued at Constantinople in the imposing hippodrome constructed under Septimius Severus and improved by Constantine. It held 300,000 spectators, many of whom held betting competitions which all too often degenerated into violent arguments and fighting.

After its origins in Rome, where the chariot was popular, horse racing spread to the Roman cities of north Africa, to France and to England. Racing as a spectator sport attained new heights of splendour in Egypt between the twelfth and fourteenth centuries. In Europe, races were staged in the main to improve the training and rationalize the selection of horses for the wars, after Canute and William the Conqueror had demonstrated the cost of relying on either the sea or the infantry as a defence against the invader.

For centuries, Galloways and other native horses were raced in England, partly for the entertainment of the people – though the early Christians were strongly opposed to racing of any sort – and partly to enable observers to assess their potential as war horses. But by the seventeenth century a lightweight and lively breed had already made its appearance on the roads and in the stables. This breed, the Arab, soon appeared on the racecourses as well. Throughout the seventeenth century Arab stallions were crossed with English mares, creating an entirely new breed – the Thoroughbred.

At the beginning of the eighteenth century the Thoroughbred was recognized as the official racehorse of England, and the Stud Book was adopted as the primary source of authentication of prospective Thoroughbred horses. All modern Thoroughbred stock is descended from three great stallions of this era – the Byerley Turk, the Godolphin Barb and the Darley Arabian.

Thoroughbred blood, in turn, contributed to the creation of the American trotting breed, the Standardbred, and the bigger-boned and sturdier steeplechaser. These three horses form the basis of the most popular forms of modern racing all over the world.

Some idea of the commercial interest shown in the modern racehorse is provided by the remarkable fees paid over the last decade for various champions: 1,000,000,000 Lit. in 1960 for Ribot (this for his hire alone); $4,800,000 in 1967 for Buckpasser; $5,000,000 in 1969 for Vaguely Noble, and $5,400,000 in 1970 for Nijinsky. In each case the price was based not only upon the value of the particular horse, but also upon that of his subsequent progeny. The transaction involves an obvious element of risk, particularly as the stallion's record at stud has yet to be proved when he retires from the racecourse; but history has proved that the champion Thoroughbred, like the champions of any other breed, produces foals of championship potential. That potential was certainly realised in the case of the foals of earlier stallions, such as the flat racehorse Eclipse, the trotter Volomite and the steeplechaser Adios. Their descendants won thousands of races, and the hearts of millions of racegoers.

What is good conformation?

The particular combination of physical attributes which distinguish a breed is set out in the stud book or register of each breed. Broadly speaking, there are three distinct groups of animal – the riding animal, the draught animal and the pony, which does not exceed 14.2 hands in height. The riding horse and the pony possess the same characteristics; but the draught horse has a different, more sturdy make, shape and action to enable him to pull heavy loads rather than carrying weight at speed.

In the riding horse, quality is all-important, and so are the limbs. A horse with insufficient bone or malformed limbs may be likened to a table with rickety legs. It will not be able to fulfil its job in life with any semblance of adequacy. Good feet and limbs are an essential, indeed, in any sort of horse, whatever its purpose.

Quality shows itself first in the head, secondly in the limbs and feet, and thirdly in the general proportions and the coat, and the hair of mane and tail. A quality horse has a lean, bony head, free from fleshiness, and finely-chiselled. The head, which should terminate in a small, neat muzzle, sensitive and mobile, with nostrils capable of wide dilation to permit deep and rapid inhalation of air, may be square and tapering, like that of the Arab horse; blunt, as in the Breton; arched or Roman, as in the Barb. The fashion of the arched head was promoted in France, in the second half of the eighteenth century, by the Comtesse du Barry, who altered the profile of the Norman horse, which in turn inherited it from the Frederiksborg, and is now in the process of losing it once more with frequent infusions of Thoroughbred blood. The blunt head of the Belgian, which resembles a rhinoceros, must be regarded as defective, as must the long, thin, bony, old-looking head of the Western Friesian, and the bird-like head with high, close-set eyes of the old Hanoverian breed.

The shape of the nose and face is often one of the most distinctive features of the breed – the dished face of the Arab, the straight face of the Thoroughbred, or the convex or Roman nose which generally denotes lack of breeding. The forehead should be long and wide – foals always have a convex brow, but this characteristic in the mature animal often implies a bad temperament, especially if it is combined with a small, piggy eye. The eyes should be large, dark, limpid and set level with the head, neither sunken nor bulging, though the latter is preferable to the former. The horse can see sideways past its shoulder, while the lines of forward vision should cross on the muzzle.

The neck should be wide at its base, nicely turned or curved on its upper side or crest, and should form a right-angle with the head. If its upper line is too convex it is known as a 'swan neck', and if it is concave it is said to be 'upside down' or a 'ewe neck'. It should be of moderate length, neither too long nor too short, and should run into a well laid-back, nicely sloping shoulder. A horse with a straight shoulder is not only invariably a bad mover, for all movement of the front limbs should come from the shoulder, but it is an abomination to ride. A straight shoulder is only forgivable in a harness horse.

Ears should be widely spaced, neat and light, very mobile and moderately long – except in the pony, which should have small ears – and should be pricked and held in a forward position. A great deal can be deduced about a horse's character from the way in which he carries his ears. If they are mobile and carried forward he is usually

The numbers on the left-hand diagram show the points of the horse; the numbers on the right relate to the exterior parts of the body.

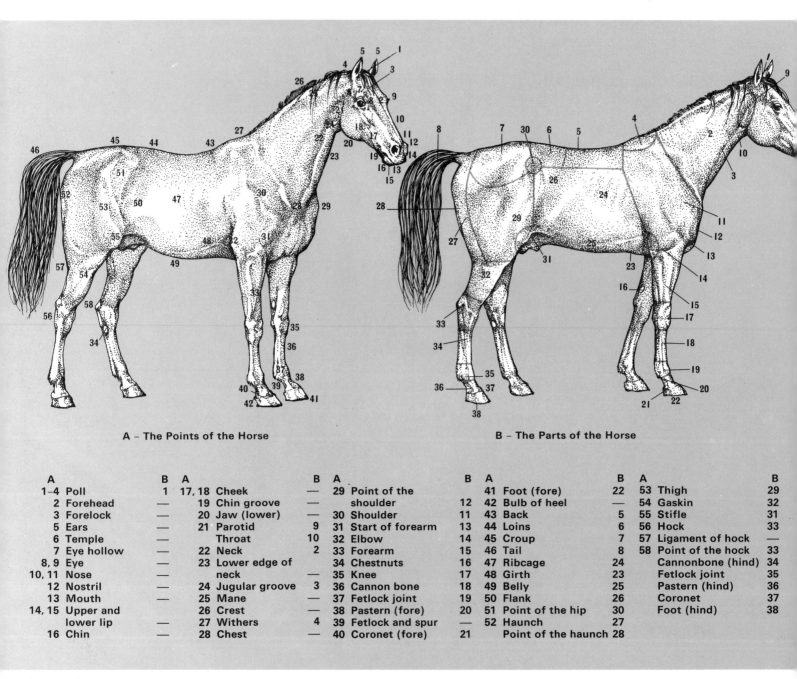

A – The Points of the Horse

B – The Parts of the Horse

A		B	A		B	A		B	A		B	A		B
1–4	Poll	1	17, 18	Cheek	—	29	Point of the		41	Foot (fore)	22	53	Thigh	29
2	Forehead	—	19	Chin groove	—		shoulder	12	42	Bulb of heel	—	54	Gaskin	32
3	Forelock	—	20	Jaw (lower)	—	30	Shoulder	11	43	Back	5	55	Stifle	31
5	Ears	—	21	Parotid	9	31	Start of forearm	13	44	Loins	6	56	Hock	33
6	Temple	—		Throat	10	32	Elbow	14	45	Croup	7	57	Ligament of hock	—
7	Eye hollow	—	22	Neck	2	33	Forearm	15	46	Tail	8	58	Point of the hock	33
8, 9	Eye	—	23	Lower edge of		34	Chestnuts	16	47	Ribcage	24		Cannonbone (hind)	34
10, 11	Nose	—		neck	—	35	Knee	17	48	Girth	23		Fetlock joint	35
12	Nostril	—	24	Jugular groove	3	36	Cannon bone	18	49	Belly	25		Pastern (hind)	36
13	Mouth	—	25	Mane	—	37	Fetlock joint	19	50	Flank	26		Coronet	37
14, 15	Upper and		26	Crest	—	38	Pastern (fore)	20	51	Point of the hip	30		Foot (hind)	38
	lower lip	—	27	Withers	4	39	Fetlock and spur	—	52	Haunch	27			
16	Chin	—	28	Chest	—	40	Coronet (fore)	21		Point of the haunch	28			

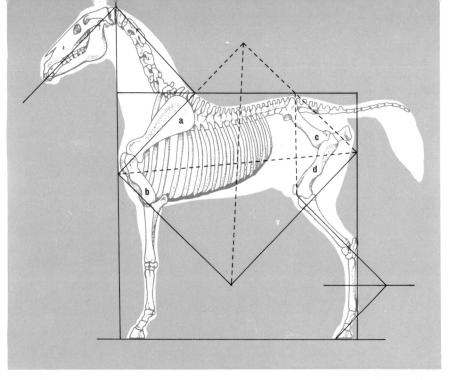

intelligent and kindly. If they are habitually laid back he is almost certainly bad tempered, and untrustworthy.

The mane should be fine, neither too thick nor too sparse. An erect mane is a characteristic of the ancient breeds, and is typical of Przewalski's horse, while a thick, soft mane which falls on either side of the neck is a feature of the Shetland pony. The colour of the mane may also be a definitive point in certain breeds. For example, the Avelignese and the Palomino have a mane that is lighter than the basic colour of the coat, while the Fjording has an erect mane of two colours. Coarse, wiry hair goes with a common,

underbred animal, and more so if it is kinky. A flowing mane is usually brushed to the right, to fall on the off-side of the neck, opposite to that on which the rider mounts, though in some countries it is brushed and trained to lie on the near-side.

A wide and open chest is a sign of strength, and it is very important that a horse should not give the impression of narrowness when viewed from the front or he will be deficient in stamina. The broad chest of the draught horse is well adapted to exerting a strong pull on the collar or harness, but it is just as important in the riding horse as it implies good heart and lung room. This is also denoted by depth through the girth – one of the most essential attributes of a horse who needs stamina and staying power, such as the steeple-chaser, the hunter and the three-day event horse.

The shoulders should be oblique and particularly well-muscled in all riding horses. A sloping shoulder is a joy to sit behind, a straight one purgatory. The wither should be well defined and of moderate height and width. A flat wither reduces the leverage from the neck and usually goes with a shoulder that is loaded with fat, so that the saddle keeps coming forward and requires a crupper to keep it in place, as on some fat ponies. The high, thin, knife-like wither requires a specially designed saddle and is susceptible to galls which are difficult to heal and keep the horse out of work. Once formed, these galls are very liable to recur under the slightest pressure, even from a stable rug.

The forearms should be strong and well muscled, the knees wide and flat and slightly

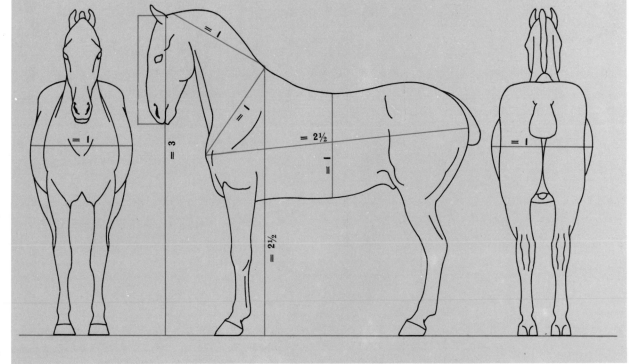

convex. Concave knees are a definite weakness and place undue strain on the tendons. A horse that is 'over at the knee' almost never breaks down, but a horse with knees like a calf – 'back at of the knee' – is naturally disposed to unsoundnesses of the lower leg. For the same reason, the cannon bone which connects the knee to the fetlock joint should be short, and the tendons behind it should be hard and clearly defined. Any coarseness or thickening is a sign of impending trouble.

The fetlock joint, too, should be hard and cool, without fleshy swellings such as windgalls. Round joints do not stand up to work. The pastern which leads down to the hoof should be of moderate length and slope. Too long a pastern, though it gives a comfortable, springy ride, is a weakness. Too short and upright a pastern is unable to absorb sufficient concussion and again produces a rather uncomfortable ride.

The coronet band, at the top of the hoof, and the hoof itself should be hard, strong and even-surfaced. The foot should be open and straight in its surface, neither long and boxy, like that of a donkey, nor flat as a soup plate, which indicates dropped soles. As they have to support a greater weight, the front feet are generally slightly wider than the hind feet.

When the foot is picked up the frog, which absorbs concussion, should be big and well-developed and in contact with the ground. If it is small and shrivelled, as it can be in the long, narrow, boxy foot, it is unable to carry out its function and foot trouble will not be far away. The feet and the flexor tendons which run down the back of the lower leg are the most vulnerable points of the horse – the latter particularly for the

22

The forerunner of our own domestic donkey is the Nubian Ass, photographed here in Somalia. It has characteristic stripes on its legs and the dorsal lines known as Saint Andrew's cross. Below: An onager with its foal.

racehorse, the hunter or the event horse or show jumper, which is subjected to continual violent exertion. Once the tendons are badly strained or torn, the working life of the racehorse comes to an end and he is said to have 'broken down', though in recent years an operation has been performed on bowed tendons with great success.

The legs between knee and fetlock should be straight and vertical to the ground. Viewed from the front, they should turn neither in nor out. If they do, it will lead to faulty action, and though a horse that 'toes out' is merely unsightly, a horse that 'toes in' can knock himself and even, in extreme cases, bring himself down.

The back should be horizontal – though in an old horse, or one which has been worked too young, it may dip in the centre – and it should be wide and muscular. A short back denotes strength, but a slightly longer back gives a more comfortable ride and enables the horse to cover, and to stand over, more ground. The muscular development of the back has considerable bearing on its length. A horse with a wide expanse of weak or slack loin behind the saddle is generally lacking in stamina and a strong constitution. If the loins are on the long side but well muscled up, they are not so objectionable. The racehorse can be forgiven a longer back than, for example, the draught horse, as it enables him to extend himself further, denoting good scope, without the danger of his over-reaching, which is striking the foreleg with the hind shoe.

The loins, then, should be wide, comparatively short and well coupled into the pelvis, thus enabling the horse to transmit the whole propelling force of the hindquarters. In some draught breeds, muscular hypertrophy produces a kind of central furrow.

The rump should also be well muscled, and should carry only a moderate slope. The flat rump of the Arab and of some types of German horse is preferable to the steep downward slope towards the tail, which is called 'goose-rumped' and is another sign of weakness. Although the horse which has his tail 'on top of his back' is the ideal, but is not found that often, a tail which starts too low is generally accompanied by thoroughly weak hindquarters.

According to Arab belief, the rump or croup should be as long as the combined length of the back and flanks. A large, muscular rump of great width is characteristic of draught horses, which

The Connemara pony has Andalusian blood and therefore also some Arab blood—the breed is believed to have originated from horses which reached the Irish shores after the shipwreck of the 'Invincible' Armada in 1588.

25

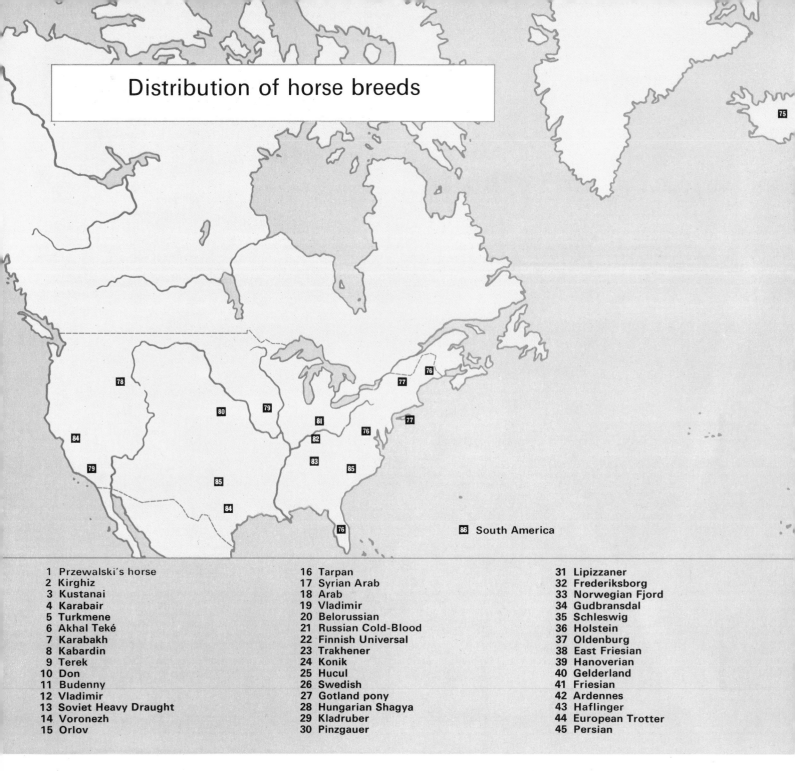

Distribution of horse breeds

1 Przewalski's horse	16 Tarpan	31 Lipizzaner
2 Kirghiz	17 Syrian Arab	32 Frederiksborg
3 Kustanai	18 Arab	33 Norwegian Fjord
4 Karabair	19 Vladimir	34 Gudbransdal
5 Turkmene	20 Belorussian	35 Schleswig
6 Akhal Teké	21 Russian Cold-Blood	36 Holstein
7 Karabakh	22 Finnish Universal	37 Oldenburg
8 Kabardin	23 Trakhener	38 East Friesian
9 Terek	24 Konik	39 Hanoverian
10 Don	25 Hucul	40 Gelderland
11 Budenny	26 Swedish	41 Friesian
12 Vladimir	27 Gotland pony	42 Ardennes
13 Soviet Heavy Draught	28 Hungarian Shagya	43 Haflinger
14 Voronezh	29 Kladruber	44 European Trotter
15 Orlov	30 Pinzgauer	45 Persian

gives them their typical rolling gait, while the more elegant but less solid, horizontal rump is typical of the racing trotter. Flat-race horses and steeplechasers have a moderately slanting rump.

The tail should be soft and fairly thick, carried high and proudly, almost on a horizontal line with the rump when the horse is in motion. The primary function of the tail, which is nevertheless an adornment, is to flick off flies and other insects.

The thorax, which encloses the lungs and heart, should be wide and deep, with a well-rounded rib cage to accommodate a maximum respiratory capacity. The abdomen should be cylindrical, and small enough to prevent the intestines from pressing on the diaphragm and limiting pulmonary

expansion. For this reason, racehorses are given a high calorie, nutritive diet of concentrates with a high protein content, and less bulk feed such as hay.

A horse with true and correct proportions is a beautiful animal, whatever his breed. When the mechanics are perfect, the horse has a lovely action or – more properly in the riding horse – movement. The Arabs regard their horse as the masterpiece of creation, and tabled his requirements as follows: that he should have pure eyes, skin, head and feet; short ears, flanks and cannon bones; long neck, abdomen, haunches and legs; and wide brow, chest, rump and pasterns. Of all modern horses, the one to come nearest to this

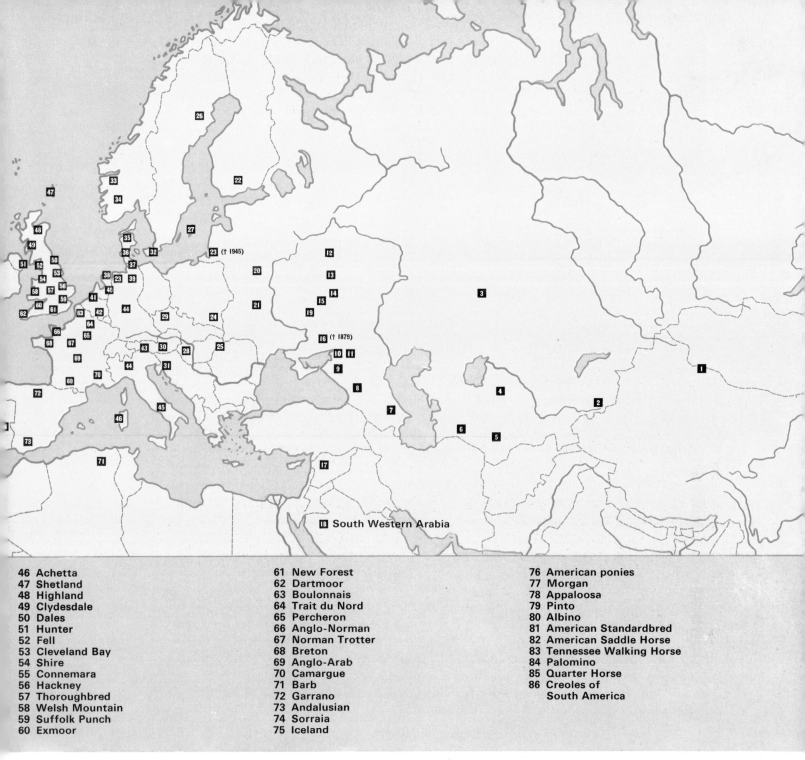

46 Achetta	61 New Forest	76 American ponies
47 Shetland	62 Dartmoor	77 Morgan
48 Highland	63 Boulonnais	78 Appaloosa
49 Clydesdale	64 Trait du Nord	79 Pinto
50 Dales	65 Percheron	80 Albino
51 Hunter	66 Anglo-Norman	81 American Standardbred
52 Fell	67 Norman Trotter	82 American Saddle Horse
53 Cleveland Bay	68 Breton	83 Tennessee Walking Horse
54 Shire	69 Anglo-Arab	84 Palomino
55 Connemara	70 Camargue	85 Quarter Horse
56 Hackney	71 Barb	86 Creoles of
57 Thoroughbred	72 Garrano	South America
58 Welsh Mountain	73 Andalusian	
59 Suffolk Punch	74 Sorraia	
60 Exmoor	75 Iceland	

The distribution of horse breeds from East to West, from the founder of the species, Przewalski's horse (on the borders of Mongolia and China), to the new breeds of the United States. The horse reappeared in America only 480 years ago, after an absence of millions of years, with the invasion of the Spanish 'Conquistadores.'

description is the Thoroughbred.

English and Irish breeders, indeed, consider that the Thoroughbred is a better-made animal than the Arab, whose shoulders are too upright, giving him a short front, and whose hind-legs are too bent in the shape of a sickle for their liking. They set great store by the shape of the hind leg, in particular the hocks; this is, after all, the 'engine'. Hocks which are hooked are liable to strain in the form of curbs, spavins and thorough-pins. They aim for a strong and muscular second thigh, a large bony hock, free from fleshiness, and they like the hind leg to drop straight down to the ground from the hock, with no forward curve, so that a straight plumbline can be dropped ver-

tically from the tail to the ground which will touch the point of the hock and the fetlock joint. This is the type of hind leg which has proved to be the most durable in the hunting field and on the steeplechase course.

Characteristic signs

The coat of a horse is not enough, in itself, to identify a breed, but some breeds have a coat texture or colour which is an important and necessary feature. The most notable examples are:–

White coat (white hair on pink skin) – the

American Albino.

Grey (white hair on dark skin) – the Camargue ponies, Lipizzaner, Orlov and Percheron.

Bay in its various shades – the Cleveland, Sorraia, the horses of Poitou.

Light mane/tail – the Avelignese and the Palomino.

Spotted – the Appaloosa, the Knabstrup and the Pinzgauer.

Dun – Przewalski's horse.

Black – the Friesian.

Gold sheen – the Karabakh and the Akhal-Teké.

There has never been a roan, a skewbald or a piebald Thoroughbred, though roans in particular are fairly widely diffused among trotters and cart horses.

Among other identifying features of the breeds are: the eel stripe (dorsal stripe) typical of the Tarpan and common to many ponies: zebra markings on the legs, which almost invariably accompany the eel stripe, except in the English pony breeds: and the mealy muzzle of the Dulmen and the Exmoor pony.

One of the qualifications required for the registration of a horse as a member of its breed is size. This is represented by height at the withers, which is measured in hands from the top of the withers to the ground. A hand is equivalent to four inches. Size, and weight, are for the most part determined by heredity, environment and nutrition.

There are giants of the species, 16.2 to 17.2 hands or more and weighing a ton, like the Shire horse and the Belgian; and at the other end of the scale there is the Shetland pony, which has a height limit of 42 inches.

The trot is a two-time movement on diagonal legs. It reflects the gait of a man, walking or running: right leg and left arm forward (first movement), then left leg and right arm forward, and so on. In the 'flying trot' there is a moment when the horse is not touching the ground.

Small horses are generally known as ponies, but there is no official limit since the maximum size for a pony varies from 40 to 61 inches, depending upon the country of its origin. Most pony breeds are tougher than horses and better adapted to withstand, and even to thrive on, poor keep and harsh climates. Their endurance led to their widespread use, both during and after the industrial revolution, for heavy draught work in the coal mines. Happily, this work is now carried out by machinery and ponies no longer work underground.

The horse in sport

The use of horses for sports other than racing or hunting has shown a significant increase since the end of the Second World War, when a revival of interest in riding all over the world turned the horse from a necessity, as it was formerly, into a luxury animal. Show jumping was the first such sport to find world-wide followers, closely followed by three-day events. Now more horses are being bred than at any time since the spread and development of the internal combustion engine.

The general utility horse, usually by a Thoroughbred stallion out of a half-bred mare, is the most popular for general use, but the more accomplished the horseman, the more quality he requires. Thus the Thoroughbred has been used all over the world to impart more quality to the breeds already established. The time factor in show jumping and combined training competitions puts a premium on quality allied with substance and an equable temperament. The

29

coarser horses are generally confined to the smaller riding schools, catering mainly for novices who require a horse to be very nearly bomb-proof, and the trekking centres.

Most German horses have a natural spring and their riders exert a dominating influence over them which produces very good results. A great many German horses have found their way into the show jumping teams of many other nations, and more will undoubtedly do so following the success of the German team in the Olympic Games at Munich in 1972. The Germans have held a distinguished record in show jumping since the end of the Second World War. But many riders rather prefer the Irish Hunter, of the type of the grey Ambassador, by Nordlys, on which Graziano Mancinelli won the individual gold medal for Italy in Munich. The Italians have always been

enthusiastic buyers of the Irish horse, and to a lesser extent the English equivalent.

In the field of three-day events the British horses are supreme, and have been so ever since 1967, remaining unbeaten in every international team event including the 1968 and 1972 Olympic Games. English horses are in great demand for the international teams, and even the Germans fielded two of them in Munich, as did the Americans. These two teams respectively won the bronze and the silver medals.

Most of the English horses are sired by the premium stallions of the Hunters' Improvement and Light Horse Breeding Society, which holds an annual show for Thoroughbred stallions, most of them only recently out of training, at Newmarket each March. Here some eighty stallions are judged for their conformation, action and

The canter is a three-time movement, and the gallop is in four-time. At a gallop, over a distance of one mile, the horse is one of the fastest-moving animals, and can reach more than 38 mph with a rider in the saddle.

type, having first undergone a stringent veterinary examination to ensure that they are free from hereditary unsoundnesses or disease. Those that are awarded premiums or super-premiums (the best fourteen stallions present) are then made available to members and cover their mares at a very modest fee. The progeny have won Grand Nationals, Olympic medals, hunter championships galore and have shone in many different fields of competitive endeavour.

With the World and European junior team championships both in show jumping and in three-day events, there is an ever-increasing demand for good horses everywhere, which can only increase as leisure time increases and working weeks grow shorter. The horse provides enthusiasts with many forms of healthy exercise and recreation, and riders from seven years to seventy are discovering each year the truth of the old adage: 'There is something about the outside of a horse that is good for the inside of a man.' Though competition increases every year, there will always be many who, without ever aspiring to winning anything, just enjoy riding for its own sake. Certainly there are few better ways of relaxing, and escaping from the rush and noise and bustle of modern life, than riding a horse through the quiet of the countryside.

Those prophets of doom who once forecast the demise of the horse have been well and truly confounded, for the horse is as deeply entrenched in the lives of many thousands of people in every country as he has ever been. Deeper, perhaps, for whereas in former days he was a necessity, now people ride simply because they want to.

There is also a vast increase in the breeding of ponies, for thousands of children and young people are riding all over the world, and from families who in pre-war days would never have contemplated taking their children to a riding school. Native stock is constantly exported to France, Holland and Germany for breeding purposes from the British Isles, whose happy heritage it is to have a foundation of no fewer than nine distinct national breeds, evolved over the generations in Wales, the New Forest, on Dartmoor and Exmoor, in the Highlands of Scotland, the bogs and the mountains of Connemara, and the dales and fells of the north country.

The British Pony Club boasts a membership of over 100,000 children, and riding is just as popular in the United States, where trail rides and dude ranches provide yet another outlet. Indeed, the horse and pony, now nurtured and cherished all over the world, are in a stronger position now than in all the millions of years of their long and devious evolution.

31

Horse breeds of the world

Tarpan A horse whose history dates back to the Stone Age; together with Przewalski's horse, it is held to be the ancestor of all present-day lightweight or riding breeds. The Tarpan survived in numerous wild herds in the steppes of eastern Europe and Russia for thousands of years, but its history as a wild animal came to a close when the last Tarpan still at large was tracked down and killed at Askania Nova in 1879. Ironically, steps were immediately taken to restore the Tarpan family, the most successful attempt being made by the Polish authorities, who rounded up ponies which resembled the Tarpan in almost every detail. The Tarpan breed is now kept alive in the Polish reserves at Bialowieza and Popielno, where the herds roam in a semi-wild state. Despite the efforts of experimental breeders in Poland and at the Munich Zoo, many authorities remain convinced that the herds in existence are not true Tarpans. Nevertheless, with their bay coats, dorsal stripes and black manes and tails they bear a striking similarity to their ancestors who once roamed the steppes.

Konik A breed native to Poland, and the closest heir to the Tarpan, with which it shares a fearless temperament, great hardiness and high fertility. These qualities, among others, have endeared the Konik to the farmers of Poland and the lands which lie on its borders, by whom it is bred for agricultural use. Its breeding goes back many centuries, but it was not until the 1900s that it received official recognition and began to be conserved in its native country. Like its cousin, the Hucul, the Konik has been improved over the years with infusions of Arab blood. Despite its small stature – it stands only 13 hands high – it is considered to be a horse, rather than a pony, although it shares many traits with the latter. Colours vary between yellow dun, mouse-grey and blue dun, and some Koniks retain the dorsal stripe and zebra-markings of their wild Tarpan ancestors.

Hucul A relative of the Konik and another descendant of the Tarpan, the Hucul is the pony *par excellence* of north-east Europe. The Carpathian mountains, its stronghold for thousands of years, have produced a pony of outstanding strength and courage, ideally suited to pack and saddle work in the difficult terrain of the region. Today it is used primarily for farm work in southern Poland and the Carpathians. Arab blood has been used for grading-up here too, but the Hucul retains its primitive stamp, particularly in the shape of its characteristic Tarpan head. The colour is bay or dun, and piebalds are to be found in some areas.

Left: the much-discussed horse of the Forests (caves of Combarelles), ancestor of the cold-blooded breeds. Right: Two Przewalski's horses, in the caves of La Madeleine.

Mongolian pony, a very common breed in south-eastern Siberia. It is quiet and tireless, and very similar to the ponies on which Scott tried to reach the South Pole (1912-1913). Below: the ponies of eastern Indonesia and of Timor sometimes have Arab blood.

Przewalski's Horse This breed derives its name from the Russian explorer, Colonel Nikolai Przewalski, who discovered specimens on the western borders of the great Gobi Desert. Whether or not this horse is a part-ancestor of all modern breeds remains uncertain, but there is almost universal acceptance of the theory that it is the only truly wild horse in existence today. Sadly, its survival is being threatened increasingly by the encroachment of civilization on its traditional range, the foothills of the Yellow Wild Horse Mountains. Those few horses which still exist in the wild live in much the same way as the Mongolian wild horses of the Pleistocene age and have retained many of their distinctive features – notably the dun colour, upright mane, dorsal stripe and leg stripes. The qualities of speed and stamina, so essential in such a hostile environment, have also been preserved through the generations. It is becoming increasingly clear that, despite the efforts by the Mongolian and Chinese governments to save the breed from extinction, the fate of Przewalski's horse lies in the great zoos of Europe and North America, where there are more than 140 specimens on display to the public.

Arabian The Arabian is perhaps the most celebrated member of the horse family, famed throughout history for its beauty, elegance and purity of blood. It is almost impossible to assess the contribution and the impact made upon light horse breeding by the Arabian, such is the extent to which its blood has been used to improve stock throughout the world. All modern light breeds are related, through the Thoroughbred – which derives from Arabian stallions – to the Arabian.

The oldest and purest breed in existence today, the desert Arabian has been bred pure since 700 AD, both in its native land, the Arabian peninsula, and in countries which imported them after the Crusades. After the First World War the numbers of the pure-bred desert Arabian declined alarmingly, but the breed was saved from extinction by the continued efforts of the traditional breeders, the Bedouins, and by studs in Great Britain, Poland and the USA. It is in these three countries that the breeding of Arabians is largely centred, but Arabian Stud Books have been established in at least a dozen other countries during the present century.

The modern Arabian breed divides, through the mares, into five distinct lines or strains: Kuhaylan, Siglavy, Habdan, Hamdani and Obajan. Each line traces its ancestry back to a

A self-possessed young shepherd on his Mongolian pony.

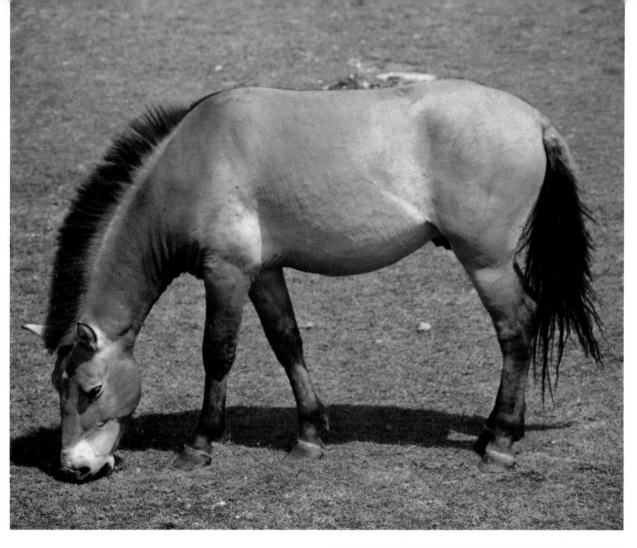

foundation mare owned originally by a sheikh or tribe. These strains retain their individual traits and characteristics, at the same time sharing those outstanding features which are common to the breed as a whole, enabling it to be distinguished so easily from lesser breeds.

Undoubtedly, the head remains as the most dominant and distinctive characteristic. Concave in profile, the head is wedge-shaped and small, tapering from a broad forehead to a narrow, delicate muzzle. The eyes are large, prominent and highly expressive, and tend to be oval rather than triangular. The beauty of the head is enhanced by its proud, high carriage. Next in order of importance, after the limbs and the hindquarters, comes the coat colour. Most modern pure-bred Arabians are grey, though the shade can vary from nearly black, in youth, to light, dappled or flea-bitten markings. Chestnuts are fairly common but bays are found less frequently in every country. Both coat and skin have a distinctive, silky texture.

The tail, like the head, is carried high as the Arabian moves in its inimitably graceful manner. It is reasonably adept at all paces, but the canter is its most beautiful and distinctive pace. As befits a horse bred through the centuries to withstand the rigours of the desert, the Arabian can draw upon remarkable resources of stamina and endurance.

A splendid Przewalski's horse: the white nose and the half-fleshy tail are characteristic of the breed. It is the only breed which is still really wild, and the sad and mistrustful expression on the face of the horse in the lower photograph bears witness to its dislike of captivity.

Above: Even at thirty years old, this Arab mare is still young, and parades her latest foal with all the pride and satisfaction of a young mother. Below: A beautiful purebred Arab. Its docility is a sign of class and distinction— it is almost as if it were born to be the lord, not the servant.

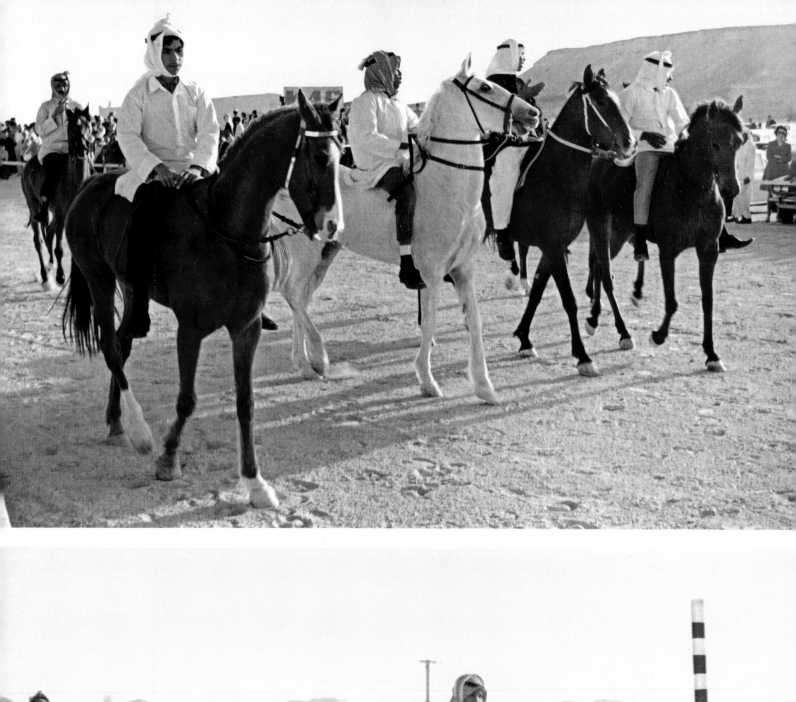

These qualities, combined with keenly-developed senses of sight and hearing, have earned their possessor an undying reputation as one of the finest performers over long distances.

Perhaps the true appeal of the Arabian lies more in its temperament and psychology than in its physical attributes. Courageous and intelligent, patient and trustworthy, teachable and good-natured, the Arabian may be said to combine all the best qualities of the horse. The true and strong influence of Arabian blood is evident in the ancestry of most modern light breeds.

Left: The Bedouins' Friday races, at Rifaa in Bahrein (Persian Gulf). Above: Blue Arabian horses are so highly prized in America that they are now registered in the 'Blue Arabian Horse Catalog'. This one has a very good pedigree.

Unlike many other breeds, there is no height restriction for the Arab horse. The average size is between 14 and 15 hands, but there are innumerable pure-bred specimens in this country and others that fall short of, or exceed, this height. Despite its considerable muscle, the Arabian is only fractionally over 1,050 lbs in weight, which makes it ideally suited to speed and agility.

Persian Arab A distinguished Oriental breed, first introduced into Persia some 4,000 years ago, its antiquity provides some justification for the belief – widespread in Persia – that the Persian Arab was the ancestor of the more famous Arab of the Middle East. Be that as it may, the Persian Arab possesses many of the features characteristic of the Arabian, notably the concave head, large eyes and high head and tail carriage. Like the

Arabian, too, the best pace is the canter. The overall appearance is one of elegance and speed. A slightly taller horse than the Arab, the Persian Arab is a native of mountain country rather than a desert horse.

Syrian Arab   An Oriental breed, also descended from the Arabian, its native territory is the Syrian desert east of Damascus. Strong and elegant, and grey in colour, the Syrian Arab is highly valued in its own country, where the government requires breeders to register all foals in the official stud book and records all pedigrees.

Some of the best racehorses have come to Europe from Syria in recent centuries. The Darley Arabian, one of the famous trio of Thoroughbred ancestors, was imported from Aleppo, having been exchanged for a hunting rifle by John Brewster Darley. Originally regarded as a pure Kuhaylan, the Darley Arabian is now recognized as a Munighi, a type which is also found in Turkey, Egypt, Iran and Iraq.

Left: The pure Barb horse is most commonly found away from the sea; this one, with all its ribbons and tassels, was photographed in Nigeria. Above: The sturdy Kurdistan pony is well adapted to the rugged mountains of the Turkish border.

Barb   A horse bred for thousands of years in the north-west corner of Africa, an area once known as Barbary, but now divided between Morocco, Algeria and Tunisia, the Barb is of great historical importance due to its influence upon the horses of Spain, which were later introduced into the Americas. Yet despite this influence, and despite the excellence of the breed as a saddle horse, the Barb is virtually unknown outside north Africa.

Even in its native territory, the modern Barb bears little resemblance to its ancient ancestor, the Barbary horse, which was bred by the Moors and famed for its staying power and its dappled coat. The Barbary horse survived the invasion and subsequent occupation of its native land by Moslems, but underwent considerable modification in its structure and substance with continued injections of Eastern blood from horses introduced by the invaders. The greatest contribution came from the desert-bred Arabian horse, from which the modern Barb derives its speed, hardiness and proud carriage.

Throughout the fifteenth, sixteenth and seventeenth centuries Barbs were exported in increasing numbers to European countries, where they soon became renowned as racehorses. In England, they were crossed with the native stock, producing many fine saddle horses, and through the legendary Godolphin Barb contributed to the evolution of the Thoroughbred. On its native heath the Barb was used to mount the French African Army during the last century, and was greatly prized in this capacity.

Generations of interbreeding with Arabian and other Oriental breeds have produced a horse of exceptional toughness and willingness, the latter marred only by bouts of bad temper, a trait which is an undoubted legacy of centuries of abuse and neglect at the hands of unknowledgeable and insensitive men. Certain characteristics of the pure-bred Barb still remain, in particular the long, 'ram-shaped' head, the flat, lean shoulders and the low tail set. To all other outward appearances, it bears a strong resemblance to the Arab.

Andalusian A breed admired throughout the world, it remained the most famous horse in Europe until the emergence of the Thoroughbred horse in the eighteenth century. The Andalusian is founded on Oriental horses brought from Morocco and Algeria by the Moors in their invasion of Spain in the eighth century. One Barb stallion, Guzman, was crossed with the local Spanish horses and ponies – including the Sorraia and the Garrano – to produce a distinct breed, the Guzmanes. From later crossings with Arabian stock sprang the Andalusian, a breed which combined all the best qualities of oriental and native Spanish blood.

The original home of the breed, as its name suggests, was Andalusia, an area whose climate and pastures are remarkably like those of parts of Arabia. By the end of the fifteenth century the breeding of the Andalusian had become concentrated in three studs established by the Carthusian monks of Seville, Jerez and Cazallo. Backed by enormous funds, the monks tended their herds with the utmost care and devotion, and it is greatly to their credit that they managed to maintain the essentially Oriental nature of the Andalusian at a time when breeding in Spain was largely influenced by the Neapolitan, and other horses of Central Europe. The Andalusian continues to be bred, together with its offshoots, the Andalusian Carthusian and the Zapatero, in studs in Andalusia.

With its vigorous and martial bearing, this was the outstanding parade horse of the Middle Ages. In that time it influenced and contributed to the establishment of other famous breeds, among them the Lipizzaner, the Friesian, the Kladruber, the Frederiksborg, the Anglo-Norman and even the Neapolitan. The modern Andalusian, though retaining its distinctive bearing and showy action, is now rarely found in its pure and homogenous form. It may be distinguished from the modern Arabian, and from most other Oriental breeds, by its straight profile and Roman nose. The principal colours are grey and black; duns and palominos may occasionally appear.

Sorraia A semi-wild horse found in the foothills of the Sierra de San Mamede in Portugal, the exceptional hardiness and adaptability of the Sorraia found favour among the cowboys and farmers of the region, who used it both for riding and for agricultural work. Despite efforts to maintain the breed, it is declining in numbers and very few pure-bred animals remain today. While essentially a coarse and undistinguished animal, it is interesting in that it possesses the zebra marks and the dorsal stripe of the primeval horses of northern Europe, and the flowing black mane. The most common colours are palomino and isabella, but greys are also to be found in certain parts.

Garrano A lightly-built pony, native to the Portuguese provinces of Garrano do Minho and Traz dos Montes, the Garrano has remained virtually unaltered throughout its history, despite infusions of Arab blood given regularly during the present century. A remarkably versatile animal, the Garrano was once run in the provincial trotting races which attracted breeders and punters from all over Portugal. Now it is used principally for agricultural work and as a dray horse, and it is in increasing demand as a pack animal for the army.

The Garrano is quite unlike other horses of the Iberian peninsula; it has a concave profile, circular eye sockets and a superior conformation, while the arrangement of its teeth is like that of the Celtic pony. In other details, especially the stocky, robust body, short legs and coarse, thick coat, it may be compared with the Exmoor pony. Again, like many of the native ponies in the United Kingdom, it varies greatly in size, some being as small as 9 hands while others are as high as 12 hands. Dark chestnut is the most usual colour.

Achetta A pony bred for centuries in the mountain regions of Sardinia, its name means literally 'of small proportions'; but it is better known among the islanders as 'Portente', which refers to its unusual gait. It is, and always has been, used almost exclusively as a means of transport in the mountains – a function which it has discharged with distinction, being agile, sure-footed and tough. Its prowess as a mountain pony went unrecognized, strange to relate, until the nineteenth century, when French military ob-

servers recommended it for use in their newly-formed Alpine cavalry.

Originally derived from heterogenous elements, the Achetta became better defined with the introduction of Barb blood in the eighteenth century. Today it is mainly crossed with Arabs and Thoroughbreds, though the former outcross tends to increase the size and spoil the structural harmony of the breed. The finest examples possess a noble profile, similar to that of the Arab, strong legs with fine bone, well-sprung ribs and good shoulders, and long pasterns which give it its characteristic, somewhat Spanish step. Chestnut, grey and bay are the most usual colours, and the temperament, though lively, is equable.

Salernitano One of the most impressive saddle horses of Europe, bred in the Salerno valley and in the Maremma, in Latium, the Salernitano – like the Calabrese, the other Italian warm-blooded horse – has surrendered pride of place in its native lands to Thoroughbreds and trotters, breeds which owe their popularity in Italy to the national preoccupation with racing. The Salernitano, in contrast, is descended from native Italian stock, its most famous and influential ancestor being the Neapolitan, of which traces can still be found in the Salernitano.

The breed started to decline in the nineteenth century, largely as a result of a ministerial decree issued in 1874, but returned to the fore some fifty years later as a luxury carriage horse and as a riding horse.

Its role changed again in recent years as the Italian school of riding increased its demand for high-class riding horses for show jumping and

A beautiful Sard horse, crossbred with English Thoroughbred blood for greater height.

From the herd to the show ring, the Maremman horse has still kept the angularity of its Barb origin. In the photograph on the right, Maremman horses in their natural habitat.

other equestrian sports. Thus many of the finest modern Salernitanos are found in the school's headquarters which are situated in Rome, where they are systematically trained to participate in national and international competitions. The Salernitano is also in demand for the army, which keeps a number of quality brood mares. The colour of the breed varies widely, and the average height is about 16 hands.

Haflinger A pony bred initially in the South Tyrol, an area restored to Italy by the Treaty of Saint-Germain in 1919 and granted autonomy by the Italian constitution of 1947, the breed takes its name from the district of Hafling, situated in the Etschlander Mountains near Merano. Despite its present association with Italy, the Haflinger is an animal which has been bred and used almost exclusively by the German-speaking peoples of South Tyrol, Bavaria and Austria.

All modern true-bred Haflingers trace back through oriental stock to the original Arab stallion, El Bedavi, which was brought to Europe by an Austrian commission but used as a stud horse by Hungarian breeders in Babolna. In the present century the Haflinger has received infusions of blood from several central European horses, the most significant contribution being made by another Austrian horse, the Noric. The mixture of Oriental and Noric blood, in conjunction with the mountain climate, undoubtedly played a major part in developing the Haflinger into a fixed breed.

The Haflinger is the archetypal all-purpose breed; while it made its name as a fast-moving pack-pony, it is equally at home as a saddle horse or in harness to light carts and sleighs, as well as in light draught work. This versatility, combined with strength, hardiness and the ability to live on poor rations make the breed ideally suited to its mountainous environment. It contrives to preserve its stamina although it lives in the most harsh climatic conditions, and this resilience, coupled with the more superficial appeal of palomino or chesnut colouring, has endeared the pony to farmers and breeders throughout the world.

The Haflinger, like its Italian relative, the Avelignese, is easily differentiated from other breeds of pony. It has a distinctly Oriental profile, large expressive eyes and an inquisitive air – characteristics all reminiscent of the Arabian. Perhaps its most distinctive feature is its workman-like hindquarters, which lends an element of incongruity to its appearance and has earned it the amusing title: 'prince in front, a peasant behind'. The legs are short, and the back and quarters

strong. The palomino or chestnut colouring contrasts beautifully with the flaxen mane and tail and the white blaze down the face. The height is usually around 14 hands.

The **Avelignese,** a slightly larger horse bred in Trentino, Venetia and the hills of central Italy, may be described as the Italian variety of Haflinger. Similar in almost every structural detail, the Avelignese shares the famous Haflinger qualities of hardiness, stamina and dedication to duty. Their functions are very similar, but the Avelignese are more often employed on draught duties.

South German Cold-Blood A horse variously termed Noriker, Pinzgauer and Oberlander, it was originally bred in the Roman province of Noricum, which corresponds to the modern Austrian states of Carinthia and Styria. In Austria, where the horse bears the name Pinzgauer, it is widely distributed over the Salzburg and Tyrol areas. The Oberlander is a lighter type, found mainly in Upper and Lower Bavaria. In these areas, the South German Cold-Blood, with its strength and its tireless pace, rivals the lighter, more sprightly Haflinger for pride of place in draught and agricultural work.

The breed was first improved by Charlemagne and then by the Archbishops of Salzburg. The increasing demand for horses by the army led to the establishment of a stud near Salzburg in 1769. There the breed was improved still further by the use of various warm-blood stallions, including the Norman, Norfolk Trotter, Thoroughbred, Holstein and Oldenburg. Judging by the present-day representatives of the breed, the most signifi-

There is a lot of Arab blood in this Trakhenen, bred in Poland. It is an excellent show-jumping horse.

cant contribution came from the Holstein and the Oldenburg, horses native to Germany.

The South German Cold-Blood is currently in use as an agricultural horse in the farmlands of central and southern Europe, the greatest demand coming from farmers in the more mountainous regions, where a horse of this weight and character is a necessity.

The breed is ideally equipped to work in the mountains; it has straight, loaded shoulders, a powerful chest, broad quarters and an indented 'saddle-back', which provides ample room for harness. The feet are compact and strong, and the legs long with good perpendiculars. The mane and tail tend to be lighter than the coat, which may be brown, bay, dun, chestnut, spotted or skewbald. The height is from 16 to 16.2 hands, and the weight about 1,600 pounds.

Lipizzaner An Austrian horse, bred since the late sixteenth century for school and parade work, it derives its name from the Austrian imperial stud at Lipizza, near Trieste. The breed is largely concentrated in Austria, but is also found – albeit to a limited extent – in other countries that once formed part of the Austro-Hungarian Empire, namely Yugoslavia and Hungary. In these countries, however, the Lipizzaner is employed primarily in agricultural and harness work.

The breed is based upon a group of brood mares brought from Polesine, of the Marinotte breed, from the Aquiliese and Veronese, and from a group of Andalusian stallions brought from Spain at the end of the sixteenth century. The breed became established with the introduction of Arabian and Barbary blood in subsequent years. The Lipizzaner family consists of six strains,

Haflinger mare and foal.

Left: The Haflinger is a docile and willing worker. Right: The noble profile and silken mane of a young Haflinger, king of the mountains.

each named after its foundation sire: Favory, Maestoso (Andalusian), Conversano, Napolitano (Neapolitan), Pluto (Frederiksborg) and Siglavy (Arabian).

The Lipizzaner's natural flair for parade was recognized as long ago as the Middle Ages, but it was not until after the Spanish Riding School was established in Vienna that the breed achieved international renown. Since then the Lipizzaner, with its elegant action, has been trained to perform the intricate movements of *haute ecole* for the public displays of horsemanship given by the School. The training period lasts for some seven years, by which time the horse will be capable of performing one or two of the most difficult movements; for each horse is a specialist, trained to do the movements for which nature has best adapted him.

Once it has mastered the basic training, the Lipizzaner is capable of performing for many years. Some have been known to give displays of a remarkably high technical standard at the age of twenty years and more.

Despite its extravagant beauty, the Lipizzaner is hardy, extremely robust and longer-living than most horses. Surprisingly, perhaps, the head lacks the elegance and quality of most of the light breeds, but the eyes are large and appealing. The influence of Arabian blood is nowhere more noticeable than in the noble, though convex head, the small, alert ears and the proud nose. The body, set off by a short, powerful neck, presents a picture of strength, with rounded quarters, heavy shoulders and short, strong legs with well-defined tendons and joints. The predominant colour is grey; bay, chestnut and brown are increasingly rare. The tail and mane are thick and luxuriant, the former well-attached and carried high. The Lipizzaner is a late maturer, but on completing its development it shows obedience, intelligence and a willingness to learn – qualities essential to success in the display ground or the covered school or riding hall. The mature horse varies from 14 to 16 hands in height.

Camargue One of the oldest and most renowned breeds of pony, its home is the Camargue region of the Rhône delta in France. The origins of the breed are not clear; some authorities believe it to be a direct descendant of the Diluvial horse discovered at Solutré, while others contend that it has an even more ancient ancestor, possibly a member of a prehistoric breed of horse. Whatever its origins, the Camargue possesses a considerable amount of Oriental blood, predominantly Barb. Crossings with Oriental stock, while modifying

Left: A Lipizzaner at the Spanish Riding School in Vienna. The breed has become closely associated with this famous school, founded in the late sixteenth century by the Archduke Charles of Austria. Right: Lipizzaners at stud farms at Piber, Austria (above), and at Lipizza in Slovenia (below). All white horses are born black, with the exception of the American Albino and the Weissborgen, which was bred especially for the court of Hanover; then they moult and lose their dark hairs. But the Lipizzaner is in no hurry and sometimes takes six years or more to moult completely.

the conformation of the pony, have brought about no change in either physical structure or colour. The present-day Camargue retains the unusual facial features and the grey colouring of its wild forebears.

Camargue ponies, together with the equally famous Camargue bulls, are confined to a reserve which forms approximately one third of the region. It consists, characteristically, very largely

of marshland which has been left uncultivated since it was reclaimed from the sea. In this watery, almost forbidding environment, the ponies roam freely in herds (manades) of forty or fifty, grazing on the rough pastures and braving the Mistral and the south winds that sweep across this corner of France. When domesticated, they are used as cow ponies to herd the Camargue steers.

With the development of the Camargue as a tourist area, the native breed faces an increasing threat of ill-treatment at the hands of visitors to this remote and romantic region. It is indeed a sad reflection on the human race that this proud, semi-wild animal, having endured for centuries the rigours of its natural environment, may now be hounded out of existence by man himself.

The long head and wide forehead of the pony, and its marvellously expressive eyes, give it an unmistakable appearance, but despite infusions of Arab blood the general conformation is no more distinguished than that of other improved light breeds. The chest and shoulders are powerful, the loins long. The coat, in varying greys, is coarse but well endowed with hair. The pony weighs around 800 pounds and ranges from 14.2 to 16 hands.

French Anglo-Arab The finest saddle-horse of France, it is regarded throughout the world as the model Anglo-Arab. The breed was created by Napoleon Bonaparte on the foundations of the Navarrin, Iberique, Bigourdan and Tarbais horses of the Pyrenean region. The Emperor set up stables in the south-west of France at Pau and Tarbes, towns which later became centres of breeding. Other studs were established in the nineteenth century at Pompadour, near Paris, and in the Limousin region of central France. The south-western studs have traditionally bred a light type for racing under saddle, while those in the north have developed a heavier, more muscular type for cross-country riding and hunting.

Breeders relied heavily on Oriental horses throughout the eighteenth century, and were forced to reintroduce Arabian and Barb blood on an even greater scale in the early nineteenth century to offset the losses sustained during the political upheavals of the period. Andalusians were also brought from Spain to revitalize breeding in the south Pyrenean region. After the establishment of the Pompadour stud in 1846, an increasing number of Thoroughbred stallions were imported from England, specifically to improve the speed of the breed. The modern product represents a mixture of Arabian and Thoroughbred blood, with the ingredients of stamina and resourcefulness inherited from the Arab, and the speed and power derived from the Thoroughbred, in almost equal measure.

The French Anglo-Arab possesses all the qualities required of a riding horse; well-balanced and supple, it has a long, easy stride and a powerful jump, though some specimens lack the scope to shine as brightly as once they did in the field of international show jumping. Its natural ability is reinforced by the strength of its legs and density of bone, good shoulders and deep chest. Colour varies widely, but there is often some degree of white markings. The horse stands around 16 hands in height.

Norman The ancient horse of Normandy, a province with one of the longest records of horse breeding in Europe, this horse was formerly

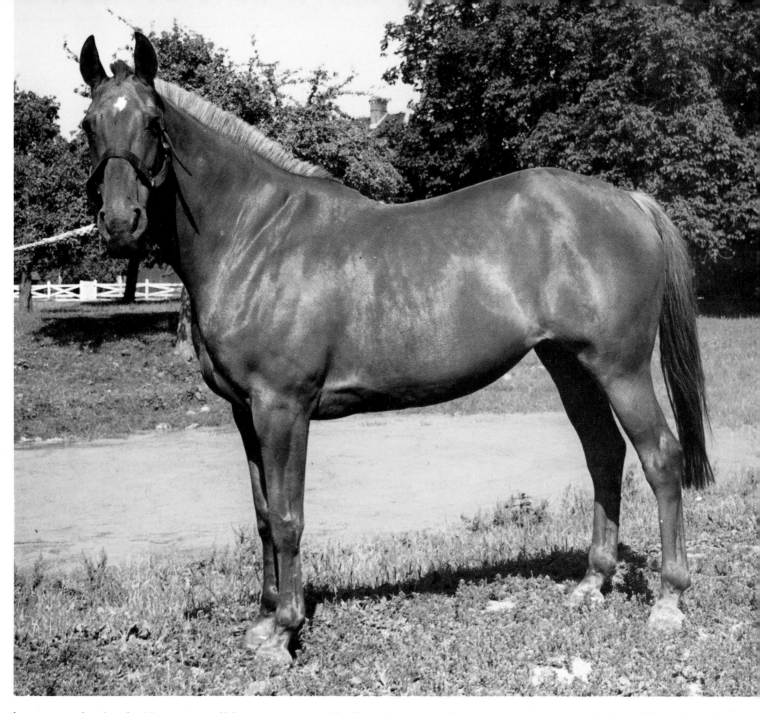

known as the Anglo-Norman until its name was changed to avoid confusion with its more famous offshoot, the Anglo-Norman Trotter. The Norman was established by the celebrated English half-bred stallion, Young Rattler, which in turn descended from the legendary Godolphin Barb. Throughout the seventeenth and eighteenth centuries the Norman was crossed with foreign breeds – the English Hunter, the Norfolk Trotter, Dutch, Arabian and Danish sires – as well as with domestic horses like the Percheron and the Breton.

The Norman attained its peak of fame during the nineteenth century when it won international recognition as one of the finest cavalry and carriage horses of its time. The horse is now bred in two types, saddle horse and cob, in the districts of Orne, La Manche and Calvados. The former, a compact, strong-legged and athletic horse, is

ideally suited to military purposes but finds its major use as a riding horse in international shows at the present time. The cob, slightly smaller and a highly active animal, is described as a heavy cavalry horse but is becoming increasingly valuable to agriculture.

Together with its blood relation, the Anglo-Norman Trotter, it has played a major part in improving other breeds in France, notably the Breton, Vendeen and Charentais. It has also contributed to the formation of separate breeds in Germany and Belgium. The distinguishing features are deep-set eyes, long and high-set ears, and a long and muscular rump. It matures late, at about six or seven years.

Anglo-Norman Trotter A branch of the older French breed, the Norman, this horse is otherwise

The Anglo-Arab was the horse chosen by Napoleon for his officers.

The Anglo-Norman is a mixture of the original Norman and a variety of English breeds.

known as the French Trotter of *Demi-Sang*, the latter title being a reference to the celebrated 'courses de demi-sang' which are staged in Normandy. The Anglo-Norman Trotter must be considered as one of the greatest triumphs of French breeding, for it has emerged from the humble origins of the little Normandy racecourses to become the aristocrat of the French trotting world. Its stock has never stood higher in the international market, and it is currently in great demand in every country where official trotting races are held.

The horse derives from three famous English stallions: the halfbred Young Rattler, The Heir of Linne (Thoroughbred) and Norfolk Phenomenon (Norfolk Trotter). Other important contributions to the breed have been provided by Arab sires, most notably Fuchsia, a distant descendant of

Young Rattler and Norfolk Phenomenon through the American Trotter, with whom it shares a common descent from the Byerley Turk, Darley Arabian and Godolphin Barb, as well as through the Norman. The stud book, opened in 1922, was closed in 1941. From January 1st 1971 the off-spring of brood mares are excluded from qualification until they reach the age of six.

Since trotting races started in France in 1836 the breed has steadily increased in numbers, and there are at present an estimated 6,000 in France alone. Among them is the fastest trotter in Europe, Jamin, which holds the record for the mile: 1 minute 59.6 seconds, set up in 1960. Although the horse is a notoriously late maturer, those with potential are given their initiation to the race-course in the special two-year-old events, which were instituted in 1950. During its career the horse may run either in harness or under saddle.

A horse of magnificent temperament, the Anglo-Norman Trotter is a powerful athlete, not yet fixed to a standard pattern, but one whose disproportions between the forehand and the hindquarters are curiously suited to the vigorous mechanics of the racing trot. Its most distinctive points may be listed as follows: long and widely-spaced ears, high withers, wide neck, low-set tail and strong, well-defined hocks. The legs are hard and fine, the feet on the large side and ideally suited for soft ground. The overall picture is that of a well-made horse combining power with elegance. The average height is 16 hands, and the horse has more substance than the American Trotter. Colours are those of the trotter generally, and white markings are found throughout the breed.

Left: At seven years old this Anglo-Arab is still only at the beginning of his show-jumping career. Right: Among Norman Trotters, the mares—the ever-popular 'reines'—are the most successful. This is 'Roquépine', born in 1961 and three times winner of the American Grand Prix (1966-67-68).

Percheron The most famous of all the present-day draught breeds throughout the world, the Percheron-Norman or Norman Percheron is an exclusively French draught horse which has been bred for centuries in La Perche, a district which lies to the south-west of Paris. The current centres are Sarthe, Loir-et-Cher and L'Orne. Established from local progenitors in the Paris basin, the Percheron was later crossed with Norman and Oriental horses, and finally with heavier European breeds. It is regarded by many experts as a composite of the Great Horse of the medieval period and the French coach horse, with an admixture of Oriental blood which has given it a small head and elegant, Arab-like contours.

Due to the irregularities in size and height among this breed, the Percheron is often divided into two distinct types: small or light carriage type, up to 16 hands and approximately 1,200 pounds; and large or great, up to and over 17 hands and 1,900 pounds or more, a type originally used for pulling city trams (cheval camionneur) and now employed to great effect in heavy draught and agricultural work. Both types display a wonderful staying power in the trot, being capable of averaging thirty-five miles a day at this gait.

The equable temperament and calm beauty of the Percheron have led to its exportation to many parts of the world. The first importer was the United States, which received its first consignment in 1839 and established, in 1905, a society (the Percheron Society of America) in honour of this gentle giant among heavy draught horses. The horse soon earned the favour of American farmers and its numbers rose steadily throughout

the nineteenth century until the 1890s, when its stock declined as a result of the depression which shook the entire nation. Breeding herds of Percherons became scattered all over the country, with the effect that superior stock were distributed over a larger area. Steps were immediately taken to revive the breed, and by 1910 almost 32,000 Percherons had been registered officially. Since then, the breed has expanded to such an extent in both the USA and Canada that it can regard North America as being virtually its second home.

Great Britain, Russia and Australia followed the USA in importing the Percheron, and the breed is now widely distributed among the major horse-using nations. In its native land it has given rise to other breeds based on local brood mares, which are quaintly referred to as 'Percherised', and to others more or less directly derived: the Trait de la Loire, Trait de Sâone-et-Loire, Gros Trait Nivernais, Trait Augeron, and Berrichon.

In spite of its bulk the Percheron is a highly nimble and energetic horse. Years of duty as a beast of burden have not in any way spoiled its natural good looks. The Percheron retains the sculptured head, with its large, lively eyes, full forehead and fine ears. Other attractive features of conformation are the full neck, muscular rump, solid legs and hard, flinty feet. The characteristic coat colour is dark grey, but other shades of grey and even black are common in some localities. The Percheron acquires its adult colour at the relatively late age of five or six years.

Boulonnais A heavy cold-blood horse, bred originally near Boulogne in France, for centuries it rivalled the Percheron in draught and agricultural work; but the decline of the breed over the present century has inevitably excluded it from any further competition in this area. The Breed is based upon the legendary heavy horse of northern Europe and, according to some sources, on the Numidian horses introduced into France by Julius Caesar. The theory that the origins of the breed lie with local mares covered by stallions abandoned by the Huns in the fifth century AD remains unconvincing.

The Boulonnais spent its early days as a war horse, reaching its height of fame in the eleventh century when it was selected by William the Conqueror for use in the invasion of Britain in 1066. Having crossed the Channel, the Boulonnais is believed to have supplied the foundations for the celebrated Norfolk Roadster or Trotter.

Une de Mai (born 1964), Roquépine's successor as the champion trotting horse, and winner of more money than any other Trotter.

Left: The muscle-man of the farm, the Percheron. It looks just as noble and fine as the Arab from which the breed is descended, despite the fact that it is twice the Arab's weight. Below: Traits Charentais in harness. Right: A young Boulonnais, less imposing, perhaps, but as noble as the Percheron.

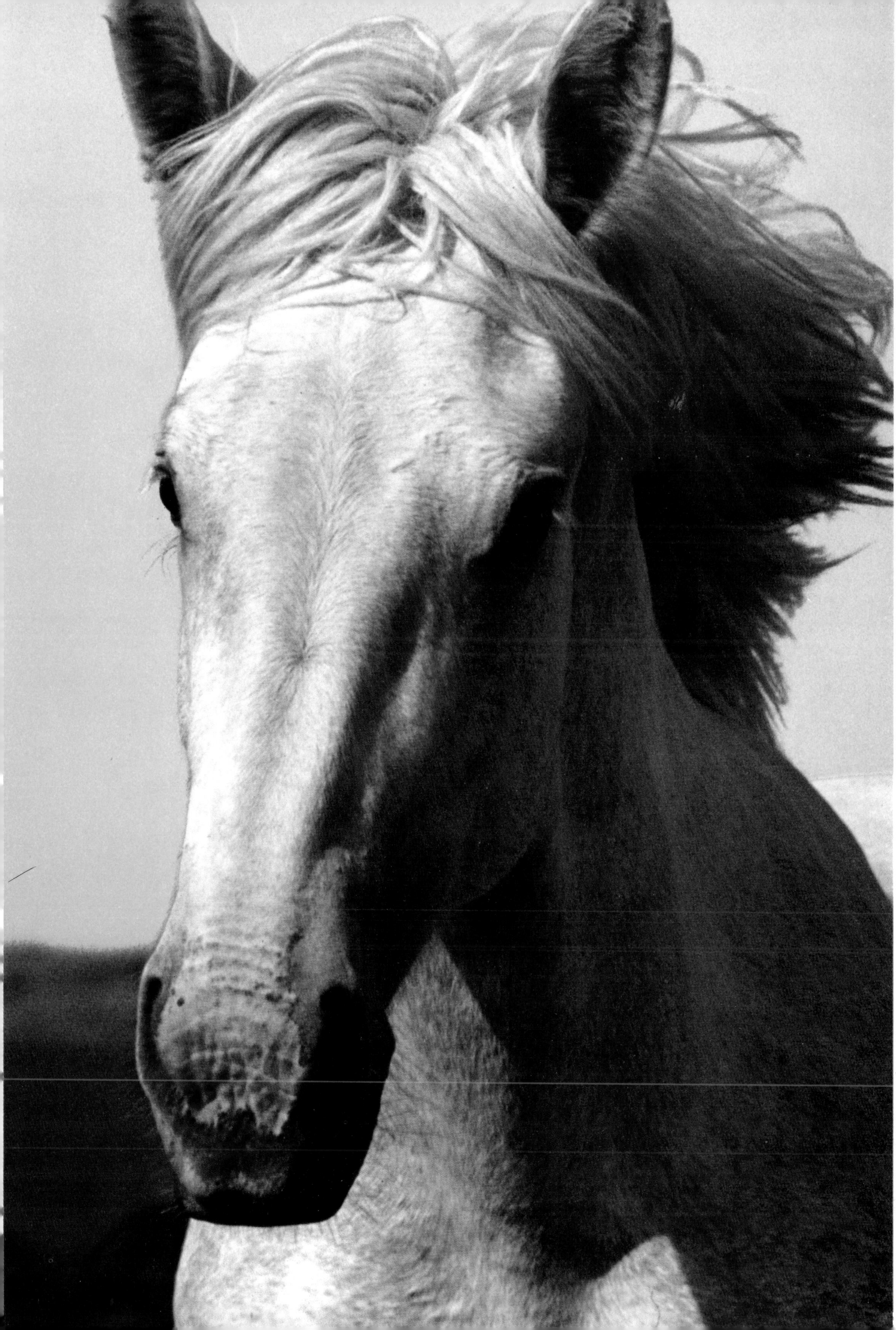

The Breton is a peasant among horses, with big shaggy fetlocks and a massive body. But it has not forgotten its days as a war-horse . . .

Gradually, the horse developed into two distinct types – the small and the great. The former, adapted to light and rapid carriage work, earned the nickname 'maréyeur' when it was used extensively to carry fresh fish from Boulogne to the markets in Paris. Sadly, both custom and horse are now fast disappearing. The great Boulonnais was used for agricultural work in northern France and such was its reputation that it has been exported all over the world, the major purchasers being North and South America.

Improved by Oriental horses since the time of the Crusades, the Boulonnais boasts the small, proud head, large eyes and wide open nostrils of the Arabian. Other features reminiscent of this noble breed are the fine skin, strong bone, clean legs and elegance of outline. Despite its bulk, this horse has an exceptional action, unusual among the northern European heavy breeds. Grey in colour, it ranges up to 16.3 hands in height and weighs around 1,400 pounds.

Breton A unique type of cart horse bred for centuries in the province of Brittany, this is currently the most popular work horse in France, being particularly prominent in areas with poor soil. There are three distinct types – the Postier Breton, a compact, clean-legged and energetic horse varying from 15 to 16 hands: the Draught Breton, a slightly smaller and less elegant animal which resembles the Suffolk Punch of England: and the Corlay (Horse of Corlay), an animal of mountain pony type, bred in the south of the province and once used under saddle in riding competitions.

Whether equipped with collar or saddle, the Breton is revered throughout the region, not least because it reflects the qualities of the Breton people: endurance, energy and colour. The principal breeding areas are Finistère, Côtes du Nord and the Midi region. At the showground at Landivisiau, in north Finistère, the best examples of the breed are displayed to buyers from all parts of the world.

To the great credit of the local breeders the Breton has managed to retain, despite its bulk, the essential character of a light cart horse, although there has been a trend, evident over the last fifty years, towards increasing weight in the draught horse. Nevertheless the Draught Breton has acquired greater bulk, and has not remained entirely immune to the movement towards increased weight, due to the use of Ardennes, Boulonnais and Percheron blood.

While still used primarily as a cart horse, the Breton has proved to be remarkably adaptable to all forms of work. This factor, coupled with its quality with infusions of Oriental and English blood over the last two hundred years, has brought a favourable response from buyers and breeders in Europe and north Africa. The colours are chestnut, bay, red roan and chestnut roan – the last being, according to local belief, the most typical and desirable.

Trait du Nord A cart horse of exceptional strength, energy and docility, members of this breed are affectionately known as 'Tracteurs' or 'Traits' in their own area of north-west France. The breed originated in Hainault, thence to spread southwards and westwards, until now it is largely concentrated in the departments of Pas-de-Calais, Aisne, Seine-et-Marne and Somme.

The Trait du Nord was originally famed as a cavalry horse, and there is some reason to believe that Julius Caesar was among those to use it in this capacity. If this be the case, there can be little doubt that the horse is of ancient origin, a belief to which many French and Belgian farmers subscribe. What is indisputable, however, is that the breed has a more recent ancestry among several giants of the species, notably the Belgian, French, Ardennes and Boulonnais.

Among its assets are an equable and docile temperament, an ability to weather the toughest conditions, and a great reserve of strength and staying power. The small, expressive head sets off a powerful body with a deep chest, full but sloping rump, short, straight back and massive legs. Colours are bay, roan and black-roan; weight ranges up to 1,500 pounds.

Belgian This heavy, cold-blooded horse is bred, as its name suggests, exclusively in Belgium. It is believed to be a descendant of the Diluvial horse of the Quaternary period, possibly through the Ardennes of France. Certainly Belgium was producing 'the Great Horse' in Brabant and Flanders in the eleventh century, areas which were almost ideally suited in terms of climate and soil to the development of a massive and powerful horse. It is from this famous type that the Belgian can claim direct descent.

Although the breed may be differentiated in three types, all display an unusual uniformity of build and general characteristics. The first and foremost type, the Belgian Heavy Draught or Brabant is an animal of enormous size and Herculean strength. Used for centuries in draught and agricultural work, it was exported to other

The Ardennes horse, too, is enormous and powerful, and can weigh nearly a ton.

European countries as long ago as the Middle Ages, thereafter to contribute to the formation of numerous other cold-blood breeds. The small, well-shaped head provides a sharp contrast with the massive body, equipped with long, fleshy shoulders, powerful haunches and large, round quarters. The legs are short but well-muscled, with feathered fetlocks. Colours are chestnut, dun or red-roan; height between 16.2 and 17 hands.

The second, and intermediate, type is the Belgian Country-Bred, an animal that has proved itself to be a highly useful working horse. It is the product of a cross between the Heavy Draught Belgian of the French Ardennes and half-bred mares, possessing some Thoroughbred blood. There is a wide variation in colour but chestnut and red-roan, characteristic of the Belgian, predominate. Height is around 16 hands.

The last type, the Belgian Ardennes, lacks the quality of the Brabant despite being its blood relation. Admired since the time of Julius Caesar, it was used centuries later by Turenne and Napoleon in their military campaigns. Many of the Belgian Ardennes were left behind in Napoleon's ill-fated retreat from Russia, and these became the basis of a local breed, now known as the Russian Ardennes. Another country to receive supplies of Belgian Ardennes was Sweden, which developed its local breed, the Swedish

Ardennes, which shares many of the characteristics of the Belgian original.

In its native land the Belgian Ardennes are to be found mainly in the north-east, where they are employed in agriculture and exhibited at the local fairs and shows. The weight of the working horse is between 1,500 and 2,000 pounds and the height approximately 16 hands or smaller.

Shire One of the famous trio of British heavy horses, with a height of 17.2 hands and a top weight of 2,425 pounds, the Shire is indisputably the colossus of the species. Traditionally associated with the Midlands, it originated in the fenlands of Cambridgeshire and Lincolnshire and claims descent from the 'great horses' of the Low Countries and native mares. Its most famous recent ancestor was the Old English Black Horse, from which it probably inherited its lively, active movement. Its heyday was the middle of the eighteenth century when, its early function as a war horse behind it, it had replaced oxen on the land and was to be found on farms throughout the shires, where it was an integral part of the countryside.

The decline of the Shire, which has now happily been averted to a surprising extent, has been accompanied by the disappearance of its most famous characteristic, the luxuriant wealth of

In the north of France, carthorses or 'traits' constitute half of the horse population, and are almost a part of the landscape.

Whether pulling a plough in the country or a cart in town, the Suffolk Punch is still holding its own in the mechanized world—and makes excellent publicity for its owners.

hair, or feather, around the fetlocks and pasterns. Breeders and farmers regard this abundance of hair as more of a hindrance than a help in most working conditions.

Black was the traditional colour for the Shire, but today four colours are recognized – black, brown, bay and grey. Average height is 17 hands, though many are bigger; and many are a ton in weight. The head is lean in proportion to the body, and forehead broad between the eyes, which are large, prominent and docile: the nostrils are thin and wide and the nose slightly Roman in outline. The ears are sharp, long and sensitive and the throat and neck clean-cut, the latter well set into oblique shoulders to give a commanding appearance. The girth is very deep, the back short and muscular, the loins well developed and packed with muscle. The hindquarters are long and

sweeping, of great width and well let down into the second thighs. The chest is also wide, the ribs round and deep, and the legs are hard and flat, with 11 to 12 inches of bone below the knee and the tendons standing out like whipcord. The pasterns have plenty of length and the feet are deep and open, while the hocks are on the straight side for leverage. The Shire moves with great force, using his knees and hocks and keeping the latter close together.

The Shire possesses all the good qualities of the ideal draught animal, and is used not only to till the fields but is to be found in increasing numbers

Next page: The biggest of all horse breeds is the Shire horse. Whatever its surroundings—drawing the Mayor's coach at the Lord Mayor's Show in London, or pulling a plough in the country—it looks dignified and self-possessed.

again in the city streets, pulling brewers' drays, railway delivery vans and coal carts. Many industries have found them to be more economical than lorries, and the few remaining breeders find a ready market for their youngsters.

Clydesdale A breed which hails from Lanarkshire and other parts of the Clyde valley in southeast Scotland, it is also widely distributed throughout the north of Ireland.

Although weighty and powerful, the Clydesdale has the best shoulders of all the British breeds, and as breeders have aimed at a minimum of superfluous tissue the general impression is of quality and weight rather than grossness and bulk. The back and quarters are packed with muscle and sinew, ribs well sprung and shoulders excellent, with high withers, whence springs a well-crested neck. Knees and hocks are big, and both feet and legs are perhaps the most remarkable feature of the breed; they are so famous for their durability that the Clyde is often crossed with other draught breeds to improve their feet and legs. The round, open feet are the pride of generations of breeders.

The Clydesdale has an exceptionally good temperament and great gaiety of carriage and outlook. Long, sloping pasterns give the characteristic springy action, and its liberty is probably derived from the galloway ancestors. A Shire lifts its feet high off the ground and shows its shoes to anyone behind – a fault in a riding horse, but not in a cart horse, whose job in life is to pull weight. The Clydesdale is among the most widely exported horses in the world, major buyers being Canada and the USA, where, in common with the Percheron and the Shire, a national association and stud book have been established in its name. The ideal colour is dark brown with the characteristic white markings dispersed throughout the body.

Suffolk The third member of the British trio of heavy horses is otherwise known as the Suffolk Punch, a reference to its 'punchy' look, provided by its bulk and compact form. While there are records to prove that the breed existed as long ago as 1506, as mentioned in William Camden's 'Britannia', it was not until the early eighteenth century that the Suffolk began to develop into a fixed breed. By careful selective breeding, its forehand, activity and outline were improved, though the prepotent characteristics remain. Every registered horse traces its descent in direct male line to an animal foaled in 1760.

Suffolks are invariably chestnut in colour and few horses, other than the Cleveland Bay, invariably breed true to colour. There are seven different shades, however, of which the most popular is the most common, a bright chestnut. Perhaps the most notable feature of all is the fact that the Suffolk is clean-legged, carrying no feather whatsoever other than a silky tuft at the fetlock, which saves a great deal of labour in the stable and also precludes the skin disease, 'grease', caused by wet fetlocks.

The average height is 16 hands, though 16.3 hands is reached quite often, and the weight varies from 2,205 to 2,405 pounds. The head is big with a broad forehead, the neck deep where the collar lies, tapering gracefully towards the head, which shows considerable quality despite its size. The shoulders are long and muscular, the middle-piece deep and compact, with well-sprung ribs. The back is short, loins and hindquarters massive and powerful, with good second thighs and a high-set tail. The knees and hocks are large and the cannon bone short and strong – indeed, one of the outstanding characteristics is the shortness of the leg. The feet are big and open and the walk smart and true, while the trot is well balanced and showy, both fore and rear. Power at the trot was well exploited in early days when Suffolks pulled the road coaches, but lighter horses eventually took over in the interests of speed and the Punch was relegated to the farm.

The breed is noted for longevity – many reach the age of thirty, and are worked until well on in their twenties – and also for their extreme kindness and docility. Although the breed has been preserved and protected in East Anglia by the Suffolk Horse Society, founded in 1877 – the same year as the Clydesdale Society and a year before the Shire Horse Society – the Punch has travelled as far afield as Russia and Germany.

Cleveland Bay One of the most famous coach horses of England, the Cleveland is a blend of riding and driving types. The breed of clean-legged Yorkshire horses, traditionally bay in colour, were used for pillion purposes in medieval times, bred in great numbers in the Cleveland district. Before the days of coaches, with the roads axle-deep in ruts, travelling for vehicles was so slow that not only did men journey on horseback, they also carried corn, coal, wool and farm produce packed on the backs of horses, which had to be strong, sure-footed, and fast walkers.

With the reign of Queen Elizabeth I came the earliest coaches, and the Cleveland was well suited to the task of drawing these heavy-wheeled vehicles. Early in the nineteenth century, John Macadam was responsible for improving road surfaces so that coaches could travel at ten miles an hour, and breeders improved the blood to

increase the pace. The Cleveland had been kept religiously free of cart horse blood, and now even more Thoroughbred blood was introduced – today, every horse registered in the stud book traces back to eighteenth-century racing sires.

Then came the railway; the coach was replaced by the carriage and pair, and so once again the mares were mated to big Thoroughbreds, the offspring (with 25 per cent of new Thoroughbred blood in their veins) becoming known as the Yorkshire Bay Coach Horse or the New Cleveland Bay, to distinguish them from the Old Cleveland Bay, a distinctly separate and ancient breed.

They found a ready world market but at the end of the last century it was found that there was too great a tendency to fine blood, and the mares were put back to the old Cleveland strains. In 1886 the Yorkshire Coach Horse Society was founded, with all purebred stallions admitted to the stud book. No drop of carting blood, however far back, was allowed, and though a strain of Thoroughbred blood could be traced in the male line, the type was fixed in the eighteenth century and has been kept clear of alien infusions ever since.

In the 1880s a great market arose for the breed in the United States, where it is still popular as a foundation stock for the breeding of heavyweight hunters. In its native land, the Cleveland is most often to be seen on occasions of state in the capital city, when many of the occupants of the Royal Mews are privileged to draw the Royal coaches.

The Cleveland stands about 16 hands, and the classic features are a long barrel, deep and sloping muscular shoulders, level and powerful quarters, a shortish back and $9–10\frac{1}{2}$ inches of bone below the knee. The colour is invariably bay, and excessive white markings disqualify a horse from registration.

Thoroughbred Although the three foundation stallions of the breed were of Eastern origin, there is very strong supporting evidence to prove that there was a distinct breed of racehorse in England before the importation of Eastern sires began, and from which some of the foundation mares originate. If this were not so, it would have been impossible to develop the breed into the supreme modern Thoroughbred in the short period of two hundred years.

A Thoroughbred is a horse that is eligible for entry in the General Stud Book, first published by Weatherbys in 1793, by tracing completely to parents who have already been accepted for registration. The first recorded horse race, how-

Sea Bird, born in France in 1962, and one of the great champions of our time.

ever, took place in 1377 between horses owned by the then Prince of Wales (later King Richard II) and the Earl of Arundel. The Tudors and Stewarts continued the fashion, and though Cromwell banned the sport, Charles II was a great supporter and may be regarded as the father of the bloodstock industry.

All modern Thoroughbreds descend from some thirty mares which were breeding in the seventeenth and early eighteenth century, and from the three imported stallions. First came the Darley Arabian in 1705, from which descend the two horses which have exerted the greatest influence upon the modern Thoroughbred: Eclipse (1764) and St. Simon (1883). Next was the Byerley Turk, whose greatest descendants were The Tetrarch (1911) and Tourbillon (1928). The third, the Godolphin Barb, was responsible for Hurry On

(1913) and the celebrated American horse, Man o' War. In the extended pedigree of any modern Thoroughbred the influence of these three original sires can be proved time and again. The Derby, St. Leger and 2,000 Guineas winner, Bahram, has no fewer than 28,332 lines to Godolphin Barb, 44,079 lines to the Darley Arabian and 64,032 lines to the Byerley Turk.

No horse can compare with the speed of the Thoroughbred – the five furlong course at Epsom, over half a mile in length, has been covered in 53.6 seconds, representing a speed of 42 miles an hour. Thoroughbred blood is used to improve native breeds in every country, and is the best source of grading-up a breed. The average height is 16.1 hands and the bone measurement below the knee should not be less than 8 inches. Bay, brown or chestnut are the most common colours.

Nijinsky, winner of the English and the Irish Derby, born in Canada in 1967.

Hunter A general term rather than a designation of breed, the Hunter is a horse of which the best specimens are to be found in England and Ireland where the sport of foxhunting still thrives. The Hunter is almost invariably the product of a Thoroughbred sire and a half-bred mare, herself by a Thoroughbred out of a mare who carries other blood in her veins as well; perhaps Irish draught, Clydesdale, native pony, or a mixture of all three. Cleveland Bay, Suffolk and Welsh Cob blood is also to be found in the back pedigree of many Hunters, though there is a tendency today for Hunters to have more and more Thoroughbred blood, to the detriment of the weight-carrying capacity of all but the best, most carefully bred specimens.

The classic Hunter is that bred in Ireland, where the combination of the good land with its lime-stone subsoil, and the foundations stock provided by the clean-legged, active Irish draught breed combine to produce a horse of great strength, stamina, jumping ability and temperament.

The English Hunter is bred by premium stallions, which are shown at the Newmarket Thoroughbred Stallion show of the Hunters' Improvement Society each March, out of native mares which often trace back to the Suffolk, the Clydesdale or the Cleveland Bay. On the whole they are less tough than their Irish counterparts, and can carry less weight. Those which are bred to carry weight often lack the quality movement, in particular the ability to gallop, of their Irish cousins which owe so much to the activity of the Irish draught horse.

Nevertheless the English Hunter is in great

71

demand overseas as an international combined training or three-day event horse; while the Irish Hunter, though almost equally good in this field, is more often exported as a show jumper.

Good shoulders, good limbs and joints, and an abundance of flat, dense bone, with good feet, are the primary requisites of the hunting horse, which may be said to be the perfect horse for riding across country. Sixteen hands is the average height, but many exceed it and a few fall some 2 inches below. Colour varies widely, but bay and brown are the most popular. Odd colours, such as piebald or skewbald, are rarely found.

Hackney The most popular breed of harness horse in Britain, the Hackney is unique among trotting horses in that it is never raced. Thus its excellence is judged not on its speed against the clock, or against others of its kind, but solely in the show ring on such attributes as quality, conformation, and above all, action.

Descended from the Darley Arabian, and related to the Bidet d'Allure, the Hackney has the Norfolk Trotter (Roadster) in its more recent ancestry, plus Thoroughbred blood; and that of the native pony, such as the Welsh Mountain and the Fell, in the case of the Hackney Pony. Organized breeding dates from 1755, and since then it has enjoyed a remarkable run of prosperity, with innumerable breeders competing to breed champions.

The qualities of the Hackney are legion. The name derives from the Norman *haquenée*, a word used to differentiate between the riding horse and the war horse. They were bred originally in Yorkshire, Norfolk and parts of Lincolnshire,

Hunters, bred specially for fox-hunting, must be fast, tireless and bold jumpers. On the left is the English Hunter, and on the right the Irish Hunter, which excels also in the show ring.

and the best could trace their descent from Shales, a son of the Thoroughbred stallion Blaze, by Flying Childers. From the middle of the nineteenth century they were in great demand as improvers of stock, and for producing carriage and military horses.

The present-day Hackney, very popular in Holland and North America as well as in England, stands from 14.3 to 15.2 hands or higher and may be bay, brown, black or chestnut, often with white markings which increase its showiness in conjunction with its unique action. The shoulders are well laid back, to assist the progressive movement, which is extravagant and spectacular. Crisp hock action is as important as high front action to the connoisseur. Limbs and feet are good and the walk is brisk and springy, and indicative of a well-muscled and active horse. The trot should be lofty, true, smooth and progressive, with the hind legs propelled forward well under the belly.

Most of the top English Hackneys now trace back to the brown stallion Mathias, born in 1895, through his son Buckley Courage. The Hackney Ponies, now considered to be a separate breed, are the result of crossing Hackney stallions with pony mares.

Dartmoor A breed of pony native to Dartmoor, in Devonshire, south-west England, it remains one of the most pleasing attractions in this wild and romantic corner of the country. The breed is preserved in a number of private studs, both in the area and beyond it, but a great many of the less show-worthy but still fairly typical ponies are to be found in the herds that roam freely over the moor.

Long accustomed to life in the wild, on a vast

and exposed tract of high land with little shelter and sparse herbiage, the Dartmoor is difficult to handle in the early stages of breaking in, but once broken it makes an ideal riding pony for the young. Years of spartan existence in this rugged country have left their mark on the breed.

The head is refined, the shoulders powerful and the limbs strong and up to a considerable weight. Bay, brown and black are the most common colours, though chestnuts and a few greys are also found. Odd colours preclude registration in the stud book and are generally attributable to the Shetland stallions which were turned out on the moor from time to time to produce a smaller pony for the coal mines. The height limit is 12.2 hands.

Exmoor The oldest of the English pony breeds, it is named after the hilly tract of moorland which borders the Bristol channel in north Somerset. There is reason to believe that the Exmoor pony had its origins in the legendary Celtic pony, used by the Celts for pack and chariotry purposes.

The Exmoor pony, like its close neighbour the Dartmoor, makes an ideal mount for children. Fleet of foot and nimble over any sort of terrain, the Exmoor has a somewhat plain head, small pointed ears, a short neck and heavy shoulders. Distinctive features are the mealy muzzle, 'toad' eye, and light hair inside the hind legs and along most of the underside. The height limit is 12.2 hands for mares and an inch higher for stallions.

New Forest The most famous resident of this scenic and still relatively unspoilt part of southern England, both the area and the breed are the responsibility of the National Trust. References

to ponies in this hilly and wooded region were made as long ago as the eleventh century, first in the reign of King Canute and then of William the Conqueror who, in 1079, claimed the Forest for the Royal Hunt.

The ponies seen in this and succeeding centuries varied considerably in size, shape and quality, as they still do today, but they formed the foundation stock for the present-day New Forester, which is gradually assuming a fixed type. Although the breed received considerable help from the Arabian stallion Zorah in the middle of the nineteenth century, the breed retains for the most part the features, including the rather plain head and cobby appearance, of its forest ancestors.

There are some two thousand ponies in their native haunt. The brood mares are highly valued as foundation stock for polo and competition ponies, as well as for the breeding of light commercial horses. Height may range from 12 to 14 hands, and colour is also very variable. The surefootedness and docility of the breed has created a wide demand for the Forester as a riding pony for all age groups.

Welsh Mountain   A pony bred, it is said, since the time of Julius Caesar, the first Welsh Mountain pony stud is believed to have been set up in Merionethshire during the Roman occupation of Britain. If this is the case, then the Welsh mountain pony can fairly claim to be the longest-established breed of all native ponies. It is certainly the most beautiful.

Its popularity owes much to the influence of Oriental blood, introduced in varying quantities over the years, from Roman times. Indeed, after nearly two thousand years, the Welsh Mountain pony may be regarded as a miniature version of the Arab horse, with the resemblance concentrated in the small, proud head with its dished face, large and expressive eyes, tiny prick ears and small, soft, tapering muzzle. The intelligence, courage and resilience which the pony manifests in every task it tackles are characteristic of the Arab but also of the native pony, which has lived for so many centuries in the harsh and cold surroundings of the mountains. Their Welsh ancestor has given them a beautiful head, a well-turned neck, well-laid riding shoulders, a proud carriage, good limbs and hard, flinty feet. Colours are grey, cream, bay, brown and chestnut, but grey predominates. There are Welsh studs in the

Above: New Forest ponies are much sought after as polo ponies. Right: The much-loved Welsh Mountain pony.

United States, where the breed is extremely popular, and in many parts of Europe, especially Holland and Germany. The Welsh Mountain pony must not exceed 12 hands in height.

The Welsh Mountain pony has provided the foundation stock for the Welsh pony of riding type, which is very like the Welsh Mountain but bigger, ranging up to 13.2 hands. This breed comprises two distinct categories – the cob-like driving pony, a compromise between the Mountain pony and the Welsh cob; and the riding-type pony. The riding pony has evolved from the use of carefully selected Arab or Thoroughbred sires of polo-pony type on the mountain mares. They are in great demand for older children because of this extra size, and they are bold, fast, and brilliant natural jumpers.

Another section of the stud book is devoted to the Welsh Cob, which stands from 14 hands to 15.1 hands. Improved by Spanish horses in the thirteenth and fourteenth centuries, in former days it was bred for trotting races as much as for work, and it has, like the Mountain pony, a very showy action which involves considerable bending of the knees and hocks. Foreign governments hold the Welsh Cob in high esteem and have taken a great many promising young sires in the past for breeding army horses and commercial stock. Gaiety and zest for life, stamina and weight-carrying capacity are inherent in the Cob, and so are the strong back and quarters for heavy work.

Fell The mountain pony of Westmorland and Cumberland, the Fell is related to the Dales pony through their common ancestor, the Celtic pony, which carried lead from the mining districts in the

The Highland pony, or Garron, is a sturdy little animal and very useful for stag hunting.

north of the Pennines and the Lake District to the smelting works, and thence to the sailing ships in the Tyne, Wear and Tees.

After the Fell Pony Society was founded just after the turn of the century, five stallion premiums were awarded by the Board of Agriculture to encourage the breeding of sturdy, weight-carrying ponies. This led to a stallion being sold to Spain, followed by others to the Argentine, the USA and India.

Black is the most frequent colour, though dark brown, bay, and occasionally grey and dun are found. The Fell is strong and hardy, with particularly good legs and feet, and carries an abundance of fine, silky hair on its legs and jaw. Shoulders are long, sloping and well-laid, the chest and loins strong and the girth deep.

Dales The Dales pony is a miniature cart horse which comes from the upper dales of Tyne, Allen, Wear and Tees, all descending from Killhope, which stands 2,200 feet above sea level. The surrounding hills of Northumberland, Durham and north-west Yorkshire were lead mining centres and the ponies carried the lead ore from the mines to the washing places in the dales, and thence into Newcastle.

The modern Dale is more powerful and cobby in build, and has lost its free shoulder action. Thus in the last hundred years it has deteriorated as a riding pony, though it is still ridden to herd sheep on the hills, and many farmers use them regularly for hunting.

Many Dales ponies are jet-black, some brown or bay, with an occasional grey; but never a chestnut or odd-coloured pony among them. They grow much fine hair on their heels and have good showy action, though they tend to go wide behind. Height is about 14.2 hands. The head is neat and full of pony character, with small ears and fine throat and jaw and a strong neck, somewhat on the short side. Shoulders tend to be straight, but backs, loins and quarters are good.

Highland A Scottish breed, the biggest and strongest of all the moorland ponies in Britain, the Highland pony breed consists of two distinct types – the pony of Barra and the Outer Isles, which is known as the Western Isle pony and ranges from 12.2 to 13.2 hands in height; and the bigger Mainland pony, which averages 14.2 hands and is used by the crofters and smallholders, and also for deerstalking, making light of a 280 lb stag. Both types are immensely strong and

The smallest, and perhaps the most endearing of all ponies: the Shetland.

Following pages: left, Shetland ponies come in all colours, but only if they are born black will they grow up snow-white like this mare. Right: Shetland ponies are used to living free and wild— this one looks rather cheeky!

well balanced, sure-footed and active over rough and boggy ground, and extremely hardy and robust.

The Highland pony is believed to have originated in northern Asia, after the Ice Age in Europe. In 1535 King James IV was presented by Louis XII of France with a selection of choice French stallions in order to increase the size of ponies bred in the Scottish Highlands. Arab blood has also been used to produce a lighter type of animal.

The dun colour, dorsal stripe and black points of the Western Isles ponies testify to the ancient origin of the pony and have never been bred out. Dun, dark cream, and mouse-dun are the most favoured colours, and zebra markings are often found on the forelegs. Blacks, browns and bays are also numerous. The coat consists of an outer layer of strong, badger-like top hairs, over a fleecy undercoat to withstand the bitter cold of the Hebridean winter.

Connemara Ireland's only native breed of pony, currently bred in the Connaught region, is another breed of great antiquity, found for centuries in the bogs and mountains that lie west of Loughs Corrib and Mask, bounded on the West by the Atlantic and on the South by Galway Bay.

Formerly both half-bred and Thoroughbred stallions had been allowed to breed indiscriminately with the native pony, but the Connemara Pony Society, formed in 1923, strove to improve the breed from within, selected a hundred mares as foundation stock and obtained a grant for the purchase of stallions from the Department of

The Irish are not outdone by the English in pony breeds. The Connemara pony is a sturdy but elegant animal, and excellent for jumping or simply for hacking.

Agriculture. The modern Connemara is consequently a very useful animal – compact and deep-bodied, short-backed and well ribbed up, with short legs, good bone, sloping shoulders and a well-balanced head and neck. Height varies from 13 to 14 hands, and though duns are less common than they were, more than half the registered ponies are grey; blacks are more numerous than bays and browns, while chestnut is not a typical colour. The Connemara has an excellent temperament and is a splendid jumper, which makes it an admirable pony for children.

Shetland A native of the Orkney and Shetland Isles, off the north coast of Scotland, the Shetland – or Sheltie, or Zetland pony – is essentially an island pony, bred in poor grazing areas under hostile weather conditions, and it has had to be tough to survive. It is the most famous of all British ponies, exported all over the world.

This pony existed in the Shetland Isles long before the earliest records were kept, and little is known of its origins. It was noted, among other small horses, by the Romans, and depicted in Spanish paintings of the Middle Ages. There were no roads in the islands until 1847, and wheeled vehicles were virtually unknown, so the ponies did all the transport jobs. In the spring, before the new grass came up, they were often forced to sustain life by eating seaweed, and mares usually foaled only every second year and suckled their foals for two winters.

The pony emerged from obscurity around the middle of the last century when ponies were first used in the pits, and the demand for small, strong animals in the coal industry reached its peak. The

Gotland mare with her foal. This breed was once threatened with extinction, but was protected by the Swedish government, and is now a great favourite with children in the Scandinavian countries.

Some attractive examples of Norwegian Dun ponies.

A young and lovely Norwegian foal.

common; grey, dun and chestnut are known, and piebalds or skewbalds are frequently seen in circuses.

The head should be as small and as short as possible, carried high, with neat little ears, a small muzzle and wide nostrils and eyes. The neck is arched and powerful, the barrel deep and round, the shoulders sloping and the withers well-defined, quarters broad and the tail set high and carried well. The undercoat is dense in winter, with long, hard hair growing through a thick, furry undercoat.

Gotland A pony native to Sweden, bred mainly on the island of Gotland in the Baltic Sea, the Gotland is known locally as the 'Skogruss'. Descended from a forest-dwelling breed of wild ponies, its most famous ancestor is the Tarpan, from which it has inherited the predominant dun colour and other characteristics of prehistoric horses.

The Gotland was almost lost to its native land as the result of wide-scale exportation to European countries earlier this century. In 1954 the Swedish government intervened and set up the Swedish Pony Association to restore some control over the breeding and care of all native ponies. Many breeders now specialize in producing Gotlands for pony trotting races, but the majority are still used for more orthodox purposes, such as farm and light harness work. Whether bred for farm or racecourse, it retains its primitive stamp through its colour, sparse mane and tail and, above all, its obstinacy. Ponies are registered at 12 hands or slightly more and weigh, on average, 400 pounds.

Norwegian One of the most celebrated ponies in northern Europe, the Norwegian is otherwise known as the Westland, Fjord or Fjording. Through countless generations it has retained the striking features of its wild ancestors in the Ice Age – cream or yellow dun colour, dark mane and tail, dorsal and leg stripes.

The Vikings were enthusiastic horseman as well as sailors, and were probably the first to breed the Norwegian pony on a large scale. Notorious as Scandinavian warriors, they are more than likely to have introduced foreign blood from horses captured and shipped home from overseas. Since the end of the Viking era the pony has been crossed with numerous alien breeds, and received infusions of Thoroughbred blood in the last century, though today the breed is sustained in purity.

A tough, industrious and obedient worker, the pony is a valuable asset to farmers throughout Scandinavia and other parts of northern Europe. Main features are a strong and compact body,

rigours of work in the mines took its toll and by 1870 the breed was faced with extinction. When the islands were almost denuded of ponies, Lord Londonderry established a special stud on the islands of Bressay and Noss to supply his own pits. He procured most of the best mares and the outstanding stallion, Jack, who was the cornerstone of the stud. Twenty years later the stud book was formed, with Jack, his sons and grandsons all registered in the first volume.

The ideal is the pony with as much weight, and standing as near to the ground, as possible; the genuine Shetland is the smallest of the species with a height limit of 42 inches at the wither. The average height is 9.3 hands; the smaller ponies are of little use and the bigger ones tend to lose the characteristics of the breed. The foundation colour is black, but brown and bay are also very

The Iceland pony is the
king of his island,
and enjoys it.
Below: Only two
breeds of ponies are
ever skewbald—the
Shetland and the
Iceland (shown here).
They are distantly
related.

deep and wide; a short, heavy neck coming out of a straight shoulder, and a broad head with deep jaws. The upright mane is clipped to shape. Height varies between 13.1 and 14.1 hands.

Iceland This pony has made such an outstanding contribution to the economic and social life of its homeland that its history is virtually the history of the Icelandic people. The pony probably arrived with the first colonists of the island, the Norwegians, in the ninth century. The influx of Celtic settlers in later centuries was accompanied by the arrival of the Shetland, Western Isles and Connemara ponies to the island, and these British breeds played their part in developing the Icelandic pony. But the breed was given little opportunity to expand until relatively recent times. The severe winters had a crippling effect upon life on the island between the thirteenth and

Iceland ponies can survive almost any hardship—in winter their fur gets so thick they look like little bears, and they search for food beneath the snow, living if necessary on seaweed and even on fish.

eighteenth centuries, taxing the endurance of both people and ponies to the full. Sadly, many ponies that had survived these centuries of hardship finally met their end in 1784, when a volcanic eruption devastated Iceland.

The modern pony is bred in two types, one specializing in draught work and the other a riding animal. The latter, possessed of remarkable surefootedness and speed, has a distinctive gait known as the 'tolt', something between a trot and a canter. Characteristic colours are grey and dun.

Friesian A horse of ancient stock bred traditionally in Friesland, Holland, it is otherwise known simply as the Dutch. Crossed with Spanish horses, in particular the Andalusian, the horse came to be known as the Harddraver, a title which may be roughly translated as 'hard trotter'.

In the Middle Ages the Friesian was a popular choice of mount for the knights of northern Europe. The breed declined dramatically in the nineteenth century, and by 1913 its numbers had been reduced to three – all stallions. The Friesian was saved from extinction by a committee which encouraged all those sympathetic to the predicament of the horse to set up special breeding societies on a regional basis. The campaign was highly successful; the Friesian population has grown considerably over the last sixty years. An undoubted key to this success was the crossing of Friesian blood with that of the German warm-blooded Oldenburg. The modern Friesian is an all-purpose working horse, equally adept at pulling heavy farm carts and working the land. It is still to be seen performing in harness and under saddle, and participating in winter in picturesque sledge and carriage races on the frozen canals.

Distinguishing features are the luxuriant mane

and tail, abundant feather on legs and joints, high action in the trot and, of course, the jet-black coat. The only white allowed is a small streak on the forehead.

East Friesian This is a German trotting horse originally bred along the same lines as its better-known neighbour, the Oldenburg. The East Friesland farmer-breeders have always placed their emphasis upon the production of a utility type and the breed has undergone many changes towards this end. The most striking was produced by the use of Arabian stallions after 1945 and more recently by the grey Hungarian stallion, Gazal. The refinement produced over the last few years by the use of Hanoverian stallions may lead to further experiments, to combine versatility with quality. The most common colour is chestnut.

Oldenburg One of the most compact and homogenous breeds in Germany today, it has been bred since the seventeenth century on the extensive grasslands of the province of Oldenburg. Founded on local brood mares, it was consolidated by the induction of blood from Andalusian, Neapolitan, Barb and halfbred stallions. Cleveland Bays, Thoroughbreds and Hanovarians in the following century brought about a marked change in the breed and produced a strong coach horse.

This in turn was replaced, after the First World War, by an all-purpose horse which enjoyed only a short run of prosperity, being superseded by the saddle horse shortly after the Second World War.

Above and right: Harddraver or Friesian. A very distinctive looking horse, once used as a war horse. They are much loved and admired throughout Holland.

This current type was so successful because of the influence of two stallions, Condor (Norman) and Lupus (Thoroughbred). The heaviest of the German warm-blooded breeds, the Oldenburg horse, while still classified as a cavalry-cum-harness type, has been highly successful as a show jumper. Its excellent temperament and its strength also suit it to all kinds of harness work. The most common colours are bay, brown and black, though the royal horses are grey. Height ranges from 16.2 to 17.2 hands.

Gelderland and Groningen Respectively the horses of southern and northern Holland; while retaining their essential differences, they tend to merge into a single type of heavy, warm-blooded breed. The Gelderland, with its Spanish and Neapolitan derivation, has established itself both as a harness horse and a show jumper; while the Groningen, a heavier animal, is used in agriculture as well as under saddle. White markings are common to both breeds, with chestnut and grey predominating among Gelderlands, and black and dark brown among the Groningen horses. Both breeds range in height from 15.2 to 16.0 hands.

Holstein A multi-purpose riding and driving horse bred for centuries in the Schleswig-Holstein peninsula, it is probable that breeding began as long ago as the twelfth century with the Marsh horse, which became one of the 'Great horses' of medieval times. A succession of Oriental, Spanish and Neapolitan stallions was introduced in the sixteenth and seventeenth centuries to add considerable quality to the breed, but the horses that

Left and right: the Holstein is rich in noble blood, and is continually improving; it is now beginning to be used for show-jumping.

were to exert the greatest influence were the English and the Yorkshire Coach Horses, which were used throughout the nineteenth century. The former helped to produce a horse with a shorter leg and an ability to gallop, while the coach horses brought the high gait and equable temperament to the Holstein.

The wide-scale use of both English and German Thoroughbreds over the last forty or fifty years has served to bring about a further change, so that the horse began to command attention as a high-class carriage and riding animal. It was sufficiently versatile to jump, gallop and win international competitions up to Olympic standard, as well as working on the land. The modern Holstein is notable for its long stride, admirable conformation and abundant bone. Colours tend to be brown, bay-brown or black, and the height limit

is 16.2 hands. In recent years the Holstein has been somewhat eclipsed by the Hanoverian because of the latter's greater speed and lighter frame.

Schleswig Heavy Draught The most popular horse in the province of Schleswig-Holstein, with its admixture of Thoroughbred and Suffolk blood, this horse has much in common with its Danish neighbour, the Jutland.

The modern Schleswig-Holstein is a heavy cob type, much used in agriculture in this part of the Federal Republic. The Schleswiger, as it is popularly termed, is distinguished by its compact low-slung body, crested neck, flat ribs and feet, and light mane and tail. The presence of Thoroughbred blood is confirmed by its lively disposition and active gait. Chestnuts predominate, and the average height is 15.3 hands.

Døle-Gubrandsdal The only heavy breed indigenous to Norway, its original home was the valley of the Gudbrands, but breeding has now largely shifted to the districts of Tröndheim, Tröndelag and Östlandet. The Døle is the result of cross-breeding between native ponies and Frederiksborg, Thoroughbred and trotter stallions. The greatest single contribution came from the Thoroughbred stallion Blader, a descendant of the celebrated Odin.

With its long, strong shoulders, luxuriant mane and tail and black or brown coloration, it is related to the Friesian horse of the Netherlands and the English Fell pony. Weight is an unstable feature, and may be anything between 1,400 and 1,500 pounds. Height varies between 14.3 and 15.2 hands.

The close relation of the Døle-Gubrandsdal is the Døle Trotter, which is of mixed ancestry. Excellent in harness, the forte of this large pony is the trot, as its nomenclature might suggest. This strong point is inherited from various European horses used to improve the breed in the latter part of the last century. The Døle is renowned for its steadiness and stamina. Colours are bay, brown and chestnut, and height is about 15 hands.

North Swedish A curious amalgam, like the Døle, of warm and cold-blood qualities, this is nevertheless regarded as a cold-blooded horse. Its line may be traced back to ancient Scandinavian ponies which lived in the northern part of the peninsula. In the nineteenth century breeding was haphazard and irregular, but this improvident attitude was brought to an abrupt halt in 1890 when the future of the breed was clearly in jeopardy due to the indiscriminate use of foreign stock. Since this time the North Swedish horse has enjoyed a remarkable revival, and can claim superiority over many other north European horses on the scores of constitution, energy and longevity. Usual colours are dun with black points, chestnut and brown, and average height is 15.1 hands.

Finnish Universal Another horse bred in two types, one for trotting races and the other – the Finnish Draught – for work in farm and forest; the breed arose from outcrossings of local ponies, still to be seen in coastal areas, with cold and warm-blooded horses especially imported from overseas. The majority of breeding is concentrated upon the Gulf of Bothnia. The black colouring, once characteristic of the breed, has given way in recent

The horse can live anywhere, from polar regions to the Equator. Here is a beautiful Northern Trotting horse.

94

years to brown and bay with white markings. The Finnish Draught weighs around 1,300 pounds, and is some 100 pounds heavier than the trotting type.

Frederiksborg This most noble and ancient of Danish warm-blooded breeds was established by Frederick II in 1562 from Andalusian and Neapolitan stock. It takes its name from the royal castle and stables which are situated twenty miles north of Copenhagen in glorious surroundings. The Frederiksborg is renowned as a carriage horse and has performed magnificently in innumerable galas and ceremonial parades.

Both the Orlov and the Lipizzaner, which are distinguished horses in their own right, owe something to this royal animal. Known for centuries as the Danish, the horse was at one time abandoned in its own stud with the closure of the royal stables. Later, with the introduction of Arab and English Thoroughbred blood, it came back into use and is still in demand as a luxury carriage horse.

Lively and good-natured, it has a spectacular trot and gallop, a small and noble head, a profile that is often slightly Roman, a well-set neck and shoulder, unpronounced withers and a full, wide rump. There is plenty of space for harness and the ribs are well rounded, though the front limbs are mediocre and the feet on the small side, but well shaped. Colour is almost invariably chestnut; height ranges from 16 to 17 hands.

East Prussian This horse comes from Trakhenen, the grandiose breeding stud which was founded by Frederick the Great of Prussia in 1732 in Lithuania as part of a campaign to enable the Prussian army to buy home-bred horses instead of buying their horses abroad. The East Prussian is one of the most celebrated horses in military history. In the nineteenth century it was unrivalled in its ability to cover the ground at a speed infinitely superior to that of other cavalries.

A lightweight type was developed for riding purposes, while a heavier horse was used to pull the artillery. Created for war, it met its fate in battle when the German Army staged its retreat from Russia in the terrible winter of 1944–5. Many of the horses were abandoned, later to be rounded up by the Russians. These formed the basis for a new breed, the Masuro, which has since become a popular draught horse in Poland and East Ger-

Riding has suddenly become a much more popular sport all over Europe. On the left, an English cross-breed in Sweden; on the right a Hanoverian in Italy.

many. Those which survived the long trek back to Germany were adopted by private studs in the post-war years to establish the present-day Trakhenen – East Prussian – breed.

Originally based on local breeds, before the Teutonic knights imported the first horses of Oriental stock in the sixteenth century, its largest infusion of Arab and English Thoroughbred blood came in 1787, when Trakhenen was adopted as the state stud.

The East Prussian has great purity of form, a fine and noble head, a long and quality neck, good shoulders and a strong back. It is a good mover and stands from 16 to 16.3 hands. Colour is usually chestnut, bay or black.

Hanoverian   This is an equally famous horse, but with a longer history than the Trakhenen. For centuries it had been depicted at the centre of the coat of arms of the city of Hanover and, until relatively recent years, could be seen pictured in pairs under the eaves of the roofs of the town houses – a tradition dating from 1714, when the Hanovers ascended the English throne. At that time there was a widespread infusion of English Thoroughbred blood among the existing breeds, and in 1735 the breeding stables of Zell were founded, a little to the north-east of Hanover.

In addition to Thoroughbred blood, Trakhenen characteristics are also dominant, due to the influence of the stallion Semper Idem. Evolved as a carriage horse of the Holstein type, and now a typical riding horse which has proved highly successful in competitive international events, particularly show jumping, the Hanoverian retains its aptitude for light draught work.

A horse of noble stamp with a distinguished outlook, it is energetic and vigorous in the trot, a good galloper and well adapted to jumping. Among the distinctive features are strong bone structure, long and sloping shoulders, muscular back, well-set tail, and strong limbs with good, hard tendons. Chestnuts predominate but bay, black and grey are also seen. Height varies from 16 to 17 hands. The stallion studs at Celle and Warendorf attract visitors from all over the world, for this is the leading breed in Germany. All the stallions are broken and trained in dressage and jumping before being used at stud.

Kladruber   A horse which developed and rose to fame alongside the Lipizzaner as a parade and coach horse, it derives its name from the celebrated Kladruby stud in Bohemia. This was established for the sole purpose of supplying horses to the Austrian court at Vienna, where the horses were maintained for state occasions. The

famous blacks of the royal mews were displayed in public for the last time at the funeral of Emperor Franz Josef in 1916.

The Kladruber was improved for the first time in 1572, when Andalusian and Neapolitan horses were introduced. The head of the grey family was the Italian stallion Pepoli, and that of the blacks was Sacramoso, a horse of the Marinotto breed. Even today the greys are generally called Generale, after a descendant of Pepoli, and the blacks Sacramoso. On the fall of the Empire the breed fell into decline but was saved from extinction by the Bohemian breeders. Having survived that turbulent period, the Kladruber prospered until the Second World War, when it suffered an equally dramatic decline, forcing breeders to introduce Oldenburg, Anglo-Norman and Hanoverian blood on a large scale. Today the Kladruber numbers four separate strains – Generale,

For centuries Hungary has produced noble and famous horses. Above, the Large Nonius; below, the Small Nonius. Facing page left, top to bottom: Furioso, Gidran and North Star. Facing page right, from the top: the long-established stud farm of Mezöhegyes, the Hungarian home of the Trakhenen, with, pictured below, its offices and stables; and, bottom, a stud farm at Gyöngyös.

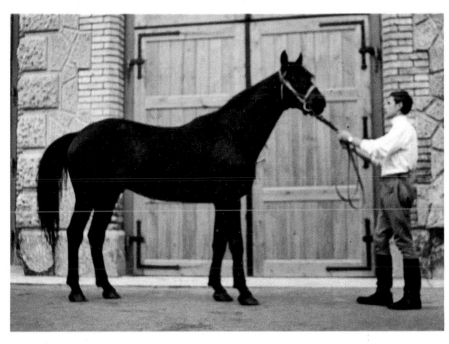

Generalissimus, Sacramoso and Favory.

A late maturer but generous, long-lived and with a sound constitution, the Kladruber has a short stride in walk and trot with pronounced action. The head is long and well-defined, with prominent eyes, a wide forehead and a Roman profile. The strong, crested neck curves away to a straight back with wide and rounded quarters. Legs and feet are solid and strong, and the height varies from 17 to 19 hands; it is one of the tallest horses in the world. The black coat of the old Kladruber carriage horse has now been replaced by various shades of grey.

Hungarian Half-bred The finest breeds of Hungary – **Nonius, Furioso,** and **Gidran** – are often referred to as half-breed animals in honour of the contribution made to their establishment by the Arab and the English Thoroughbred. Examination of the pedigree provides ample proof of their part-Thoroughbred ancestry, but some authorities object to their being described as half-bred, in the belief that the term should be applied only to a horse having one Thoroughbred parent. Be that as it may, there is no denying that the quality of these Hungarian breeds could not have been achieved without recourse to Thoroughbred blood, in whatever quantity it was given.

At the end of the last century the Austro-Hungarian Empire possessed some three and a half million horses, with Hungary alone having approximately two million. The great majority of Hungary's equine population were of 'noble' stock, with 85 per cent conventional semi-Thoroughbred, 9 per cent Norfolk-type and Lipizzaner and less than 3 per cent cold-blooded horses.

Like most other European nations, Hungary has seen its horse population declining during the present century, but its breeders have effectively reversed the trend over the last twenty years, producing some of the most beautiful horses in the world. The country also boasts one of the finest studs in Europe, Mezöhegyes, which is the main centre for the breeding of Nonius and Furioso horses. Founded in 1785 by Joseph II, the stud was reputed to have housed more than twelve thousand horses in the heyday of the Empire.

The Nonius breed takes its name from an Anglo-Norman stallion that was captured from the French stud, Rosières, after the defeat of Napoleon at Leipzig in 1813. Now bred in two types, Large Nonius and Small Nonius, this horse combines strength and hardiness with wonderful economy of movement. Major structural characteristics are the proud head, well-set neck, powerful chest and quarters. The Large Nonius, once a carriage horse of distinction, is now regarded as an all-purpose horse. A late developer, not fully mature until the age of six, it has proved to be a good choice for the formation of draught breeds. The Small Nonius, with its greater amount of Arab blood, is a horse of great stamina and good character which performs equally well under saddle and in harness.

The Mezöhegyes stud is also the home of another illustrious horse, the Furioso. This breed was established with the importation of two English stallions, Furioso (Thoroughbred) and North Star (Norfolk Trotter) in the mid-nineteenth century. Crossings of these horses with Anglo-Norman mares of the Nonius breed produced a ride-and-drive horse which soon became extremely popular in Hungary. Improved by the use of Thoroughbreds at the very end of the nineteenth century, the Furiosos were adopted for carriage work in threes, fives, and in pairs and tandems.

The Furioso, like the Nonius, is slow to mature, but it more than compensates for this shortcoming when it is fully developed into a tough, tireless horse, full of spirit. With its elegant carriage and fine head it bears all the hallmarks of the quality animal. Characteristic colours are black and brown, height is about 16 hands.

The third member of the trio is the Gidran, which takes its name from the head of the family, born in the stables of Bábolna of Oriental stock and then crossed with English Thoroughbreds. With its impeccable movement it is a saddle horse of extraordinary distinction. Lively in its work, it can be difficult to handle, but horsemen welcome

A herd at Silvásvárad stud, near Gyöngyös.

Posing for a photograph at Voronezh stud, 300 miles south of Moscow. It is one of the oldest studs in Russia, and was founded by Peter the Great.

this sort of challenge. It has a beautifully shaped head, with lively eyes and small ears. The shoulders are well formed and the upper line excellent. Colours are various shades of chestnut and height varies from 16 to 17 hands.

Russian Cold-Blood A magnificent heavy draught horse, mainly deriving from the large western cold-blood breeds through the Klepper, an ancient Baltic horse descended from the Ardennese, this horse is chiefly to be found in northern and central areas of the USSR. This vast territory provides a home for a number of other heavy draught horses, most of them bred up from western cold-blooded horses such as the Shire, Suffolk Punch and Brabant. The more famous representatives of this group are the **White Russian, Vladimir, Voronezh, Russian Heavy Draught** and **Soviet Cold-blood.**

The White Russian is a strongly built and industrious horse, combining warm and cold blood; it descends from the horse of the Forests crossed with the Breton, Norfolk, Døle-Gubrandsdal and Arabian. A splendid harness horse, the White Russian is comparatively small for its job in life – around 15 hands – and comes in a variety of colours.

Perhaps the most famous is the Vladimir, a solid and energetic animal hailing from the Vladimir region, east of Moscow. The breed developed after the Revolution when the state stud horses were used to cross the local elements with imported stallions such as the Percheron, Ardennese, Cleveland Bay and Suffolk. These crossings produced a horse of remarkable strength and constitution, qualities that were soon exploited by

From the stables of Ter, near Moscow: Tsimer, a ten-year-old half-bred with the characteristics of the Akhal-Teké.

102

the Russian farmers. The ability of the Vladimir to pull heavy loads has earned for it the soubriquet of 'the tractor horse' in its native land. The preferred colour is chestnut, distinctive features being the heavy mane and forelock and feather on the legs. Size is between 15.3 and 16 hands.

A more ancient breed is the Voronezh, which dates back to the time of Peter the Great (1672–1725). Based on local mares crossed with Dutch stallions imported to Voronezh in the late seventeenth century, in the two succeeding centuries the horse was known as the Bitjug, being dispersed along the Bitjug tributary of the River Don. Further crossings with the Western cold-blooded horses took place at the end of the nineteenth century, but some of the qualities of the old Voronezh were restored with the use of the Orlov at the turn of the century. Of symmetrical pro-

portions, the Voronezh has a noble head, large lively eyes, a luxuriant mane and straight forelegs. Walk and trot are natural paces, despite the cow-hocks which are the worst feature of the breed. A variety of colours are seen; height varies from 15 to 16 hands.

Slightly smaller but equally valuable is the Russian Heavy Draught, a lively and hardy horse distributed over a wide belt running from the Ukraine to Archangel. It has evolved from crossings of Ukrainian mares with Percherons, Swedish Ardennes, Belgian and Orlov stallions. It excels in pulling the heaviest loads at both walk and trot. This workhorse is thick-set and cobby, with a small head, massive neck and wide and muscular back. Short legs and good, hard feet give the horse a remarkable balance on rough ground.

To the north of the Ukraine lives another superb walker and trotter, the Soviet Cold-Blood. This is a relatively recent addition to the Russian breeds, established after the Revolution by crossing native mares with the Belgian. This vigorous horse serves a dual function, as a work horse used widely by the farmers in the area and at the state studs to improve the local stock. Colours are chestnut and bay, maximum height 16 hands.

Orlov Trotter The Orlov Trotter has achieved more than even its creator could have dared to dream of, having dominated the Russian trotting races, sweeping aside the finest foreign opposition and finally being recognized as the fastest trotter in the world. Its supremacy in the sporting arena lasted for a hundred years or more before the American Trotter or Standard-bred, bred specifi-

Left: Tornese (1952-1966), the greatest champion of the Italian trotting races and perhaps one of the most famous European trotters. Below: $\frac{7}{8}$ American Standardbred and $\frac{1}{8}$ Norman Trotter, this is Crevalcore (born 1953) who was Tornese's most implacable rival. He broke the international record in New York and was given the title 'Mr 28'.

cally for the purpose, took away its crown.

Having enjoyed the patronage of aristocrats, the Orlov Trotter is now bred in more than thirty-five state studs and in countless private establishments. Breeders have made extensive use of it in the development of the Don, the European Trotter, the Torgel (an Estonian horse), Voronezh and, of course, the Orlov-Rostopchin, this last being a magnificent riding horse obtained very largely through in-breeding at the end of the nineteenth century.

Outstandingly well proportioned, and almost entirely free from unsoundnesses of bone, the Orlov Trotter is a horse of genuine quality. Still engaged in trotting races, both in sulkies and in sleighs, it is equally suited to dray and farm work. The Oriental head is supported by a long, arched neck set on medium withers and oblique, muscular shoulders. The croup is comparatively long and broad, and legs and tendons solid and strong. Colours are grey, black, and bay, but chestnuts are rare. The Orlov stud book has fixed the maximum height for the breed at 16.2 for stallions and 15.3 hands for mares.

New Russian Trotter This is the latest addition to the USSR's expanding equine population, and is variously termed the Matis Trotter, Russian Half-Bred and Russian-American Trotter. It was created in an attempt to combine the very best qualities of the two arch-rivals of the trotting track, the Orlov and the Standardbred, in one form – to produce, in short, the finest trotter in the world. The first attempt was carried out in the stables of Golozyn in 1894, and met with little success, but the experiment was repeated in 1926 under the supervision of a state commission. This second attempt brought much better results, and although no further horses were imported from the USA the breeders have contrived to achieve their goal – the production of a trotter which is superior to the original Orlov, which was first bred in 1778 by Count Alexei Orlov at the Khrenov

Stud, using an Arab stallion on a dun Dutch mare.

The Orlov-Standardbred cross is produced in three types: a heavy draught type with short legs and massive build, a medium ride-and-drive type, still strong and compact, and a racehorse with a short barrel, long legs and fine bone. Height regulations are respectively from 15 to 17 hands. The predominant colour is bay, ranging through every shade to black, but greys and chestnuts are rare.

New Russian Trotters are now bred in the same studs as the Orlov, and fulfil much the same functions as the latter. This new breed has a faster trot, in which the legs appear merely to skim the ground. The present record speed is 1 minute 14.8 seconds for the kilometre, set by Gest. Some lines show a marked preference for the pace, a trait that is undoubtedly inherited from the Standard-

The Don horse is derived from the Orlov. This is Zvjozdociot, a seven-year-old gelding.

The Budenny, one of the most successful new breeds of this century. Here is Dikson, a nine-year-old stallion.

bred. The breed is docile and willing to learn, and conformation follows that of the trotter generally.

Noram A comparative newcomer to the ranks of the trotter, and a breed which has yet to become fully established, it is otherwise known as the European Trotter. It derives from the ambition of combining the best qualities of existing trotters in a single breed – in this case, the highly-strung and spirited temperament of the American Trotter with the power and co-operation of the Norman Trotter.

The centres of Noram breeding are France, Austria and Italy. Racing records indicate that the Italians have been the most successful breeders, producing, among other champions, the legendary Tornese and Crevalcore. The former, a chestnut stallion, was placed 190 times in 210 races,

winning more than £220,000 during the course of his career. He competed with Crevalcore on more than sixty occasions. Tornese followed in the footsteps of another Italian prodigy, Vandalo (1862–1888) who carved his niche in the halls of sporting fame by defeating the Orlov champions from the Prater stables in Vienna when well past his peak, at the age of seventeen. Vandalo went on racing until he was twenty-four years old, and his name lingers on among Italian trotting enthusiasts who still express their tribute in the saying 'to go like Vandalo'.

More robust than its American cousin, the European Trotter has the added distinction of being a good jumper, and is a frequent competitor in international competitions in Europe. Its confidence and courage are boundless, reinforced by an athletic, if somewhat angular, frame.

Russian of noble blood A number of warm-blood Russian horses come into this category, many of them closely related. Rich in Arabian and English Thoroughbred blood, they are gradually attaining the quality of the classic oriental breeds.

Perhaps the best known member of this exalted company is the **Don,** which rose to fame as the mount of the Cossacks. Essentially a horse of the steppes, it is descended from the small, energetic animal known as the Mongolian-Kalmuck (the Old Don). This ancient horse was improved over the centuries by Turkmene, Persian and Karabai horses and then, at the beginning of the nineteenth century, cross-bred with the Orlov and Orlov-Rostopchin. The development was completed with infusions of Thoroughbred blood, in the 1880s. While still a riding horse of great distinction, the present-day Don is regarded – and

used – as an all-purpose type. It is noted for its toughness, stamina and activity, inherent in its bone, strong shoulders and powerful quarters. The colour is a golden chestnut and height ranges from 15.1 to 15.3 hands.

A breed of more recent origin is the **Budenny,** which was established in the military stud at Rostov in 1948 by Marshal Budenny. It was created by crossing the Don with the Thoroughbred, interbreeding which has resulted in an enviable combination of mobility, stamina and speed. Magnificent in all gaits, it also boasts exceptional jumping ability, a talent consistently displayed in steeplechasing and international competitions up to Olympic level. Outside the arena of sport, the horse is used on the farms and in state studs of the south-eastern republics.

The Akhal-Teké is one of the oldest known breeds. This is Kursant, an eight-year-old stallion.

Bay and chestnut, with gold tints, make this a most attractive horse with its neat head, curving neck, and deep, wide chest and body. The limbs are strong and clean and height varies from 15.1 to 16.1 hands.

Marshal Budenny also played a considerable part in the establishment of the **Terek** breed, which traces back to the Cossack horses and was first improved in the nineteenth century, when Count Stroganov promoted inbreeding with Kabardin stock. The new Terek, which emerged between 1925 and 1948, is altogether a different animal, due to infusions of Streletsk Arab, Don and Kabardin blood. Tereks are bred mainly in the region of Stavropol, primarily for use under saddle, though they have been proved to be highly versatile. A hardy yet docile horse, the Terek is smaller than the Budenny, standing from 15 to 15.3 hands.

Across the Caspian Sea, in the republic of Uzbekistan, is found the **Karabai,** a horse which has been widely adopted for use by the inhabitants of this mountainous area. Today it is bred in three distinct types: saddle and light carriage, saddle only, and draught. Despite their differences in function, the three types tend to be uniform in size, with stallions at 15.2 hands and mares 14.3 hands. A wonderfully hardy horse, the Karabai has a gait reminiscent of the delicacy of the Arabian. The most striking characteristic of this old breed is its fine, breedy coat and its delightful golden chestnut colour. Greys and bays are fairly common in some parts of the Uzbek district.

From the republic of Azerbaijan comes the **Karabakh,** a horse of unusual distinction with the proportions of a mountain pony and a height limit of about 14 hands. Rich in Arabian blood, the horse has played an influential role in the development of the Don and Kabardin breeds. Of sufficient speed to enter for local race meetings, it has a refined head and elegant neck, wide, alert eyes and nostrils and flat shoulders leading to a cylindrical body. Legs and feet are excellent, and mane and tail, often black, are invariably darker than the coat, which varies between chestnut, golden, dun and grey, often with the 'metallic' finish or sheen which marks many of the Russian breeds. White markings are common, as also is a dorsal stripe.

Another mountain horse is the **Kabardin,** bred in the northern Caucasus but also found in other parts of the Caucasus regions and in Armenia. Used to improve the Terek in the nineteenth century, the Kabardin was itself improved with English Thoroughbred blood after the Revolution. They are now bred in herds, in three types –

Born to challenge the winds of the desert, an Akhal-Teké photographed in Turkmenistan.

original, light and heavy. The light type is bred principally in the eastern areas. A true mountain horse with great sureness of foot, a wonderful sense of direction and any amount of stamina, it is compact and muscular with solid and hard-wearing hooves. Bay is the usual colour, and height is 15.2 hands for stallions and 14.3 hands for mares.

Another popular Russian warm-blood horse is the **Kustanai,** bred throughout the republic of Kazakhstan and of much the same size as the Kabardin. Descended from the old Kazakhs strain, the breed was crossed with the Don and Orlov-Rostopchin to produce a fine dual-purpose horse. Another type of Kustanai is also found in the republic, a horse deriving from the same foundations but crossed with the English Thoroughbred. The latter has, quite naturally, a

Above and right: These are the horses of South America, much beloved of the gauchos, to whom the horse is second only to God.

The Creole is only a pony but it is fearless, and was very valuable in battle.

more noble appearance and more quality, but it shares the strength and resilience of its Kazakh cousin. A wide variety of colours may be seen among the breed.

Further to the east, on the Chinese border, we find another horse of ancient origin, the **Kirghiz.** Native to the Kirghiz republic, it is the result of cross-breeding the old Kirghiz with Don or Thoroughbred stock. Possessed of exceptional hardiness and stamina, they are bred almost exclusively for saddle and pack use in the mountains. Colours tend to be dark, height varies from 15.3 to 14.3 hands.

Of all the Russian warm-blood stock, the horse with the longest history is the **Turkmene,** an elegant animal bred for centuries in Turkmenistan which borders the south-eastern waters of the Caspian Sea. Its great antiquity, in addition to its uncanny likeness to the Munighi Arabian, provides valid grounds for the theory that it is the ancestor of the Arabian and other Oriental breeds. Whatever doubts may surround its claim to this unique distinction, historical records show that the Turkmene is the direct ancestor of another equally famous Russian horse, the Akhal-Teké, and an improver of some of the finest breeds in the USSR and Persia. The Turkmene was also crossed with the Munighi Arabian to produce the legendary Darley Arabian, one of the trio of stallions which formed the original pillars of the Thoroughbred breed.

Turkmene horses are now bred, principally for racing purposes, at the collective farm in Ashkhabad. Their speed, endurance and courage are dominant qualities. They are found in two distinct colours: bay and brown, with white markings and a golden tint, or grey, black and dun tinted with silver. Height averages 15.2 hands.

The steppes of Turkmenistan have also produced the **Akhal-Teké,** most famous offspring of the Turkmene. Perhaps the most fascinating of all the Russian breeds of horse, it was prized in the days of Alexander the Great and crossed with Oriental mares in the fifteenth century. Over the last hundred years it has received repeated infusions of blood from other horses of noble stock in order to maintain the characteristics of a horse of the steppes.

These horses are found over an area far wider than Turkmenistan, being bred in all the Soviet republics between the Caspian Sea and China, in northern Caucasia and the extreme south-west of Kazakhstan. With its subtle, copper or bronze-toned colouring, the Akhal-Teké has a dashing beauty of a type between the Arabian and the Thoroughbred. It has a rhythmic, elastic walk, a good gallop and an exceptional flair for the pace.

The neck is long and slender, the withers high, croup prominent, chest somewhat narrow, feet small and hard. The fine skin and silky hair provide the classic sign of quality. Mane and tail are sparse in hair. Height is 15.2 hands for stallions, 15 hands for mares.

No account of the horses of Turkmenistan would be complete without mention of the **Jomud,** a horse closely related to the Akhal-Teké. Well adapted to the hot, arid climate of this part of the world, it is used both to ride and drive, and is equally at home in light draught work. Arabian grey is a prominent colour in many parts, and size ranges from 14.2 to 15.2 hands.

Creoles The horses of South and Central America descended from the domestic horses which arrived with Christopher Columbus at Haiti (1493), with Pedro de Mendoza in the Rio de la Plata (1535) and with Alvar Nunez in Paraguay (1541), as well as with the streams of Spanish settlers who followed in their wake. These European horses, many of them derived from Oriental antecedents, thrived in their new environment, taking especially well to the pampas where they soon increased in number to form some of the largest herds in the world. Some, however, escaped, to make up feral bands that roamed the length and breadth of that unpopulated land.

Today the Creoles, which form the most dense equine population in the world, with one horse to every seven human inhabitants, live in a semi-wild state, many being rounded up periodically to be worked by the cowboys on the cattle ranches.

While the present-day Creoles show considerable variation in colour, size and gait (the last characteristic being shared by all descendants of Portuguese and Spanish stock), they have much in common, most notably an apparently inherent immunity to equine illnesses, considerable staying power, and an ability to adapt to all kinds of country.

One of the most resilient members of this group is the **Chilean Creole,** a horse first recognized in the Pacific War of 1879–1883, fought by Chile and the allied nations of Peru and Bolivia. Now bred in two types, the conventional pony and a smaller, 12-hand version, the Chilean Creole is derived from the Argentine.

Better known than its Chilean relation, the **Argentine Creole** is widely distributed over the South American continent, where it is renowned for its endurance and strength. Young Argentine stallions are entered for endurance tests that last for thirty days and reach their climax in a thirty-mile stretch over the most difficult terrain. The Argentine is easily distinguished from other

The Paraguayan Cr
is a typical herd hors
It is descended most
from the Andalusian

112

Left: One of the most popular contests of the rodeo is lassooing. Below: The Quarter Horse gets its name from being extremely fast over the quarter-mile race. It has been much used in western films.

Creoles by its size, about 15 hands, and colour, which may be bay, chestnut or mouse dun, with mule striping. There are an infinite number of gradations in colour, ranging from bay with dorsal stripe and black points, to strawberry roan, wine roan (Colorado Pink), to a dark coat with white markings (Nevada).

To the north is found the **Brazilian Creole,** which is divided into three groups: Crioulo do Rio Grande do Sul, a military-type pony also used for riding; Mangalarga, a descendant of a stallion of the celebrated Portuguese breed, Alter Real, introduced by Peter II, Emperor of Brazil (1825–1889); and Campolina, a heavy draught animal bred up from the Andalusian and named after its creator, Cassiano Campolina.

Returning to the Pacific coast we find the most celebrated saddle horse of South America, the **Peruvian Creole.** Otherwise known as Salteno, this breed is also divided into three types: the Morochuco, a pony used in the Andes; the Chola, a hand larger and used for farm work in the valleys; and the Costeño, which stands 15 hands high and is greatly admired for its long-stepping gait, called Paso Llano.

Travelling north-east from Peru we encounter a Creole which bears a close resemblance to the Andalusian Barbary. This is the Llanero, or **Venezuelan Creole,** a prairie horse which is often bred in herds, and is characterized by a somewhat flat structure, lightweight legs and dark mane and tail, some 15.2 hands in height. Similar in type and shape but slightly smaller is the **Columbian Creole,** a horse which has for a long time been traditionally bred in the northern peninsula of Guajira by the Indios.

Quarter Horse The oldest breed of horses in the USA, it is believed to have originated in the 1660s. It dominated the short-distance races that were much in vogue in Virginia and the Carolinas in the colonial era. Such was its success in one event, run over a distance of some 440 yards, that the English colonists came to christen it the Quarter Horse, which name it has retained ever since. With the rise of longer-distance races the Quarter Horse receded into the background and its place in the limelight was taken by the Thoroughbred and Standardbred.

The breed eventually found a welcome in the south-western states, where the cowboys and frontiersmen put it to work on the extensive ranges. It soon became very popular with the cattle ranchers, who found it ideal for stock work and for guarding their herds. With the evolution of that peculiarly American institution, the rodeo, the Quarter Horse recovered much of its old glory, displaying its consummate skill in the colourful events of the rodeo ring – barrel racing, cutting, roping, bulldogging and lassooing.

The Quarter Horse is thus a breed of great versatility, a rare quality which encouraged Americans to found, in 1940, the American Quarter Horse Association to promote the breed. During its brief history it has managed to establish the Quarter Horse as one of the most fashionable in the country, with over ten thousand registered each year.

An energetic, well-balanced animal, the Quarter Horse is a composite of Thoroughbred, Spanish and native blood. Its best known sire was an English stallion, Janus, introduced into the United States in 1756. The most striking features of the breed are powerful, sloping shoulders, heavy quarters, deep and wide hocks, good bone and an abundance of muscle. All solid colours, with the addition of buckskin, smoky and palomino are permitted; piebalds are not. Height ranges from 14.2 to 15.2 hands.

Pinto Another popular American horse, whose name derives from the Spanish word meaning painted, it is otherwise known as the Pintado. The Pinto is in fact a dappled or piebald horse, descended from stock originally introduced into Mexico by Hernando Cortez in 1519. The breed established itself in Central America before progressing northwards into the United States. Many Pinto horses that made the journey were eventually captured by Indians, who bred them in their

Solidity, agility and balance are the main qualities needed in equestrian sports, such as the gymkhana.

117

villages, leaving imprints and designs on their coats as a means of identification.

Over the centuries, the Pinto has received blood from many of the most select horses in the world, including the Barb, Arabian, Thoroughbred, Saddlebred and Hackney. The family founders of the present-day Pinto are the stallions Sheik and Sun Cloud. The stud book, opened in 1963, classifies the Pinto in three types on the basis of colour pattern. They are the Overo type, roan, chestnut or mouse-dun overlaid with white markings: Tobiano, or white overlaid with dark markings, with white mane and tail; and Morocco, again white overlaid with dark markings but with a white star on the forehead and white legs.

Like most horses bred and raised by the Indians, the Pinto is extremely docile and may, for this reason, be safely entrusted to a child for use under saddle or in harness. Its forte is the gallop, and the horse is capable of moving at a great speed if well schooled. With its delightful colouring, magnificent build and lively eyes, it can lay strong claim to being America's most attractive horse. Pintos qualify for registration at 14.2 to 15.3 hands.

Appaloosa This is a breed which has often been confused with the Pinto, due to its mottled patterns. It takes its name from the Palouse River, which runs through Washington and Idaho. Bred for centuries by the Nez Percé Indians, it was first discovered by white men when the famous explorers, Lewis and Clark, saw it on their joint expedition of 1804–1806. But it remained unknown outside the New World until the late nineteenth century, when it was displayed in exhibitions throughout Europe by Buffalo Bill.

Two lovely Morocco Pintos, a colourful breed much used in western films.

Its line traces back through Spanish stock to the ancient breeds of Fergana, an area which now forms part of the USSR. Since the breed society was founded several foreign horses, including the Arabian, have been used to improve the breed. Today it is of stock-horse type, with a long and muscular neck, deep but narrow chest and long, oblique shoulder. The colouring is the most striking feature, and divides the breed into six distinct types. They are: frost – white hairs mixed at the roots with black roan and roan; leopard – spots of various shapes; marble – dark with white mottling or veining; snowflake or spotted blanket – white spots of various sizes and shapes, on a dark background; and white blanket – grey. Foals usually assume these colours with maturity, but in combinations that differ substantially from those of their parents.

Palomino Another colour breed which is in great demand in the USA, the horse is of unknown ancestry, though clearly it is of Arab stamp. It takes its name from the Spanish conquistador, Don Juan de Palomino, probably a comrade of Cortez. The colour is one of the most admired of all, with shades of yellow or gold providing a vivid contrast with the white or silver mane and tail. The colour does not, however, breed true.

Palominos, like the Pinto and Appaloosa, are classified according to colour and are registered by two associations, whose requirements differ only in minor respects. The more famous organization is the Palomino Horse Association, founded in 1935. An ideal horse for junior and senior riders, the Palomino reached its zenith when it represented the United States in the team events of the 1968 Olympic Games, providing the ultimate

proof of its versatility. It is esteemed not only for its colour but for its regal bearing. It moves easily into the trot, holding its head proudly and disporting itself with great self-assurance and dignity. Size varies from 14.2 to 16.2 hands.

American Albino One of the best-known horses, reputed to be the only pure white horses in existence, the foals are born white and retain this appearance throughout their lives. The name Albino is, however, something of a misnomer, since the eyes tend to be blue, brown or hazel rather than pink.

The breed dates back to 1906, when a mating between an Arabian and a Morgan produced Old King, a milk-white stallion with pink skin and brown eyes. The development of the breed owes much to the efforts of one man, Cal Thompson, who established the very first Albino stud at Naper, Nebraska, in 1937. He and other, later breeders have succeeded in cultivating animals admirably suited to the requirements of public display. Their agility and spirit, quite apart from their unique colour, make them a top attraction in the circus and other spectacular forms of entertainment. Extraordinarily healthy and long-lived, the Albino is now bred in two types: the standard Albino, which stands between 14.1 and 16.2 hands, and a pony type (outcrossed to pony mares) of between 9.2 and 12.2 hands.

American Saddle Horse This is the principal show horse of the United States, distinctive for its rich repertoire of gaits, animation and style. Otherwise known as the American Saddlebred, it is acclaimed by many as a masterpiece, yet

Left and right: The Appaloosa, one of the very few spotted breeds, and perhaps the most attractive. Note the typical short tail. It was Buffalo Bill who made this breed so popular.

Appaloosa foal—the spotted coat has not yet completely appeared.

condemned by others as a parody of breeding. Indeed, it has never failed to cause controversy since the first steps were taken to shape it into a distinct breed.

In its short history it has drawn on horses of recognized style and beauty, among them the Thoroughbred, Arabian, Morgan and Standard-bred, adding to the amalgam a dash of blood from pacers and easy riding horses.

In the show ring they are exhibited under flat saddles and perform either as three-gaited or five-gaited horses. The former type have their mane and tail clipped and specialize in the walk, trot and canter, while the latter, sporting full mane and tail, perform the same gaits with the addition of the rack (a gait in four-time) and a slow gait, which may be the stepping pace, fox-trot or running walk.

121

Sioux Indians on their 'mysterious dogs'.

Apart from their unique action and style, they are easily distinguished from other light breeds by the roundness of shoulder, gracefully arched neck and remarkably clean-cut limbs. Colours are bay, black, chestnut and grey, and white markings, if not extensive, are permissible. Size varies from 14 to 16.2 hands.

Tennessee Walking Horse   This horse, the pride of Tennessee breeders, has acquired much of its versatility and virtuosity from the American Saddlebred, but it also owes a great deal to other Western breeds, including the Morgan, Standardbred and Thoroughbred, which all contributed to its formation. The greatest single contribution came from a Standardbred stallion, Allan F-I, born in the late nineteenth century.

The speciality of the breed is the running walk, a gait in which the front foot hits the ground a split second before the diagonal hind foot, and the hind feet overtake the footprints of the forefeet. This pace is so convenient, comfortable and efficient that the horse, named 'Free and Easy' after an ancestor, was sent in very considerable numbers to the sugar cane plantations of the southern States, where it became known as the Plantation Walking Horse.

It has a distinctive head, a kind eye, a slightly convex head, erect and muscular neck, long sloping shoulder, rounded ribs, short strong back, massive loins and quarters. The tail is carried high because of the incision of the inferior nerves, the hind legs slope backwards and are somewhat light in build. Colours are bay, black, chestnut and roan, and height varies from 15 to 16 hands.

Missouri Foxtrotting Horse   A breed which is not yet well defined, it first made its appearance at the start of the nineteenth century in Missouri and Arkansas. Its most characteristic gait, the foxtrot, also known as the 'broken gait', gave rise to the popular dance of the same name in 1912. A gait in four-time, which is performed by galloping with the forelegs and walking or trotting with the hindlegs, it keeps time also with the head, puts its feet down rhythmically and may even gnash its teeth to the same tempo. Used a great deal by cowboys, it has a horizontal profile, excellent upper line, quality limbs and somewhat straight pasterns. Colours are very varied, height ranges to an upper limit of 16 hands.

Morgan   The most widespread breed and the first to be trained for trotting races in the United States, the Morgan was created by an innkeeper,

Preceding pages: The wild Mustangs are the result of mistakes made by the Indians in their first experiments with horse breeding. They developed a fine character and individuality of their own, independent and obstinate—even if the Indians didn't appreciate it.

124

Thomas Justin Morgan who bred the founder of the family, Figure, (1790–1821), which passed into history as Justin Morgan. A very important horse, also known as the Arab of America, it occupies a central role for its blood contribution to the Albino, the American Saddlebred, the Tennessee Walking Horse and above all to the Standardbred, which has supplanted it in professional racing. The original founder of the family was the son of the English Thoroughbred, Beautiful Bay, and of a brood mare of mixed Arab-Oriental, Hackney, Harddraver and especially Fjording stock. The size and conformation confirm a strong pony influence. Modern Morgans are more elegant and larger than the originals, ranging to 15 hands.

The Morgan lends itself to general riding, to steeplechasing, to amateur races harnessed to a sulky and even to agricultural work. It has a docile nature, though it does not lack spirit; a lively and intelligent expression, large and short head, strong jaws, large distended nostrils, prominent eyes, and small ears. It has a muscular neck, low withers, a strong shoulder, wide short back, short and muscular loins, strong quarters and good limbs. Bay and dark chestnut are the principal colours and white markings on the body are not usually found.

The wonderful Palomino, with its unique colouring and graceful movement.

Everyone, at some time or other, dreams of owning a cowboy saddle. In the last few years of the nineteenth century these saddles cost the cowboys several months' salary, but they were their pride and joy. Here is a magnificent Palomino, near Altadera in California.

American Standardbred This breed includes, in one stud book, the trotter (the most frequently exported and best known in America and Europe) and the pacer, which has not yet been admitted to European racing. It derives from local brood mares, in Orange County and the State of New York, which have an aptitude for the trot. They include Morgan, Cleveland Bay, Hackney, Narragansett Pacer, and Canadian. The sire to wield the greatest influence was the English Thoroughbred, Messenger, imported in 1788.

The height of the breeders' ambition was always to produce a horse that was capable of trotting the mile in two minutes, or a kilometre in 1 minute, 14.6 seconds. The first to do so was a filly, Lou Dillon, in 1903. The greatest of all time was Greyhound, (1932–1965), whose record of 1 minute, 55 seconds was beaten by Nevele Pride in 1969 in 1 minute 54.8 seconds.

The first two minute pacer was Star Pointer in 1897, but the greatest was Dan Patch (1896–1916), nicknamed The Immortal. Excluded from racing in 1903 because of a lack of worthy opponents, he was instead exhibited in public, running against the stop watch. It is said that he ran the mile no fewer than seventy-three times in under two minutes, earning some three million dollars. The fastest was Speedy Star, who clocked 1 minute 52 seconds in 1971.

Until a century and a half ago, pacers and trotters raced together. Today they run separately; but there are champions capable of great feats in each speciality, the fastest of these being the so-called double-gaited horse Steamin'

Demon, with a record of 1 minute 59.2 seconds in the trot and 1 minute 58.8 seconds in the pace, totalling two miles in 3 minutes 58 seconds.

A horse of excellent temperament, willing and full of courage, and also suited to draught work, the Standardbred has a medium-sized head, a profile that is mainly straight, lively eyes, long ears, long sloping shoulders with plenty of muscle, a long humerus and short cannon bones. The withers are often ill-defined and the back long, with a somewhat defective transition to the hind quarters. The rump is high and sloping, the quarters strong and muscular, long hind legs with cow hocks, articulation unpronounced, long pasterns, and well-made feet that are on the large side. Bay is a common colour but chestnuts and blacks, more rarely grey and roan, are also found. Height varies from 15 to 16.2 hands.

American ponies A natural love of horses has concentrated the best breeds in the world in the United States, in addition to the original strains, conferring on the entire equine population of some two and a half million an impressive quality. After importing with considerable predilection, the best of the European ponies – Shetland, Connemara, Welsh Mountain and Hackney – the growing demand for children's ponies gave rise to a type, if not yet a breed, which is usually called the American pony. It is often spotted like the Appaloosa, and endowed with the Arab stamp which characterizes all the breeds originating in the United States. With an elegant body and plenty of substance combined with quality, it has a refined and noble head, rich and regular paces and an outstanding aptitude for galloping and jumping. Also well represented in Canada, its *paterfamilias* is the Shetland-Appaloosa cross, Black Hand. Height varies from 12 to 14.2 hands.

Bibliography

Chenevix-Trench, Charles *A History of Horsemanship*, Longmans, 1970

Glyn, Colonel Sir Richard *The World's Finest Horses and Ponies*, Harrap, 1971

Goodall, Daphne Machin *Horses of the World*, Country Life, 1968

Hope, Colonel C. E. G. *The Horseman's Manual*, Pelham Books, 1972

Macgregor-Morris, Pamela *Champion Horses and Ponies*, Macdonald, 1956

Raswan, Carl *Drinkers of the Wind*, Doubleday, New York, 1943, reprinted 1968

Ryder, Tom *The High Stepper*, J. A. Allen, 1963

Schiele, Erika *The Arab Horse in Europe*, Harrap, 1970

Summerhays, R. S. *The Observer's Book of Horses and Ponies*, Frederick Warne, 1948; latest reprint 1968